SLAYER STATS

THE COMPLETE INFOGRAPHIC GUIDE TO ALL THINGS BUFFY

SLAYER STATS

THE COMPLETE INFOGRAPHIC GUIDE TO ALL THINGS BUFFY

Simon Guerrier
and Steve O'Brien

INSIGHT EDITIONS
San Rafael, California

IN EVERY GENERATION
THERE IS A CHOSEN ONE.

SHE ALONE WILL STAND AGAINST
THE VAMPIRES, THE DEMONS,
AND THE FORCES OF DARKNESS.

SHE IS THE SLAYER.

CONTENTS

INTRODUCTION

"ARE YOU SURE THIS IS A GOOD IDEA?"
—DARLA, *1-01 WELCOME TO THE HELLMOUTH*

It's been twenty-one years since Buffy Summers staked her first vampire on TV, and this extraordinary series is now widely regarded as one of the greatest ever made. Its proudly feminist heart, laugh-out-loud lines, tear-jerking drama, knowing pop-culture savviness, and rich, sophisticated storytelling . . . For all the talk of *The Sopranos* ushering in the era of quality television, well, *Buffy* was there first!

This book is a celebration of the whole series—which is no small undertaking.

To watch all 144 episodes takes 4 days, 5 hours, 17 minutes, and 50 seconds. That's not including the time taken to load the DVDs and sit through the menu screens, let alone skip back through an episode to check important details like whether running into the door of that van in *3-09 The Wish* knocks Giles unconscious or just knocks him over.

(See page 44 for the answer to that one.)

We've dedicated *months* to watching and rewatching all the episodes to compile this exhaustive visual guide. Along the way, we've had to impose a few rules:

We've mainly focused on the 144 TV episodes of *Buffy the Vampire Slayer*, not Angel's own spin-off series or Buffy's further adventures in film, books, comics, or anywhere else.

Wherever possible, the graphics are based on hard facts and numbers provided in dialogue or action on-screen, rather than on our own opinions.

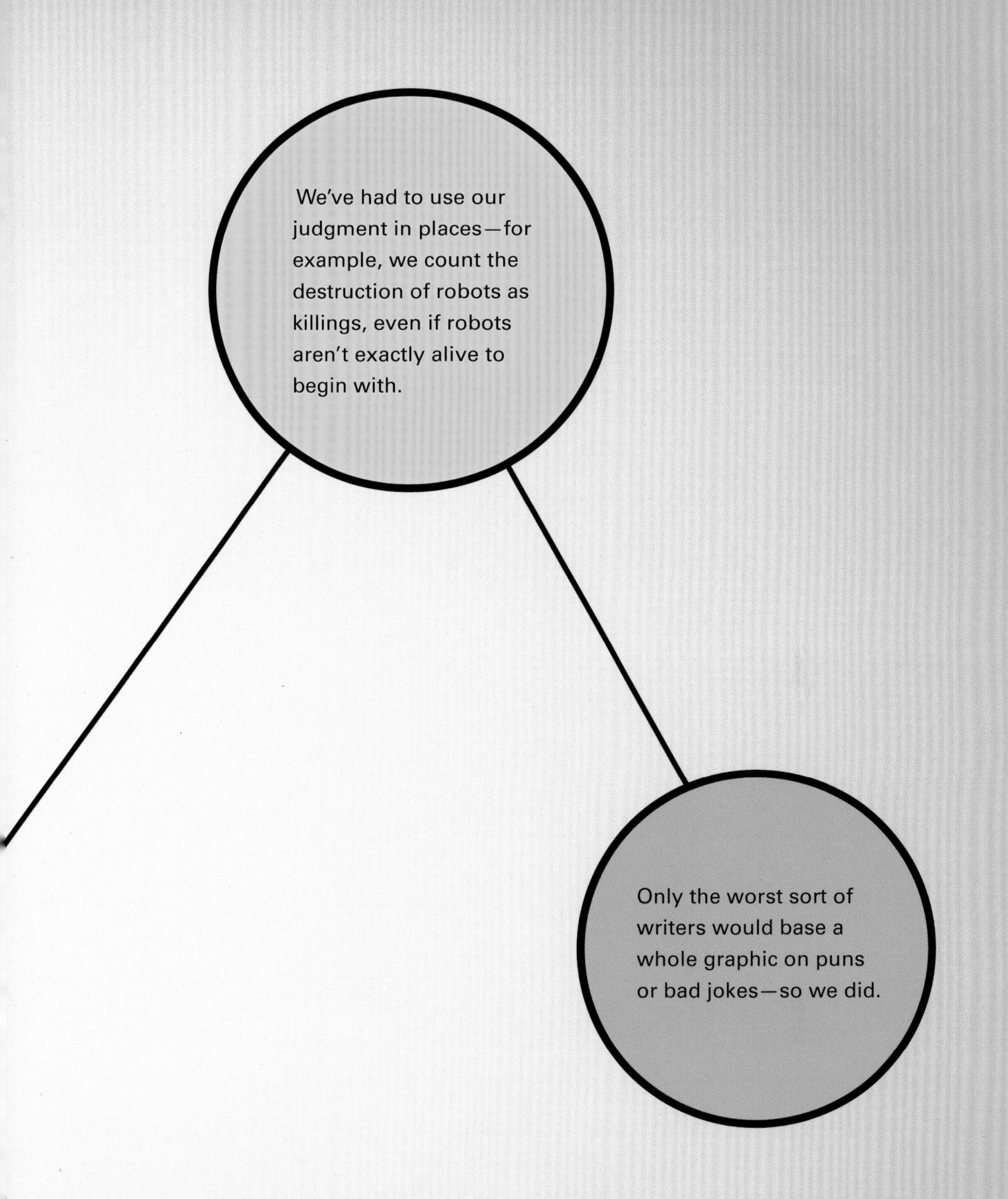

Our aim was to produce a fun, surprising, and sometimes boggling perspective on Buffy's adventures. As a result, we think we know Buffy pretty well. We've even got the evidence to suggest what she might think of what we've done:

After seven seasons on TV, Buffy has no need for Watchers anymore. Giles, her original Watcher, long-term mentor, and friend, can't tell her what to do, and the Watchers' Council of Britain has been entirely blown up. When Buffy shares her power with all the potential Slayers around the world, it seems this incredible force of young women will now fend for themselves . . .

. . . with no need for awkward, nerdy Englishmen watching what they get up to and scribbling it down in a book.

—Simon and Steve

BUFFY ANNE SUMMERS

ESSENTIAL INFORMATION ON THE CHOSEN ONE, WHO SAVES THE WORLD A LOT

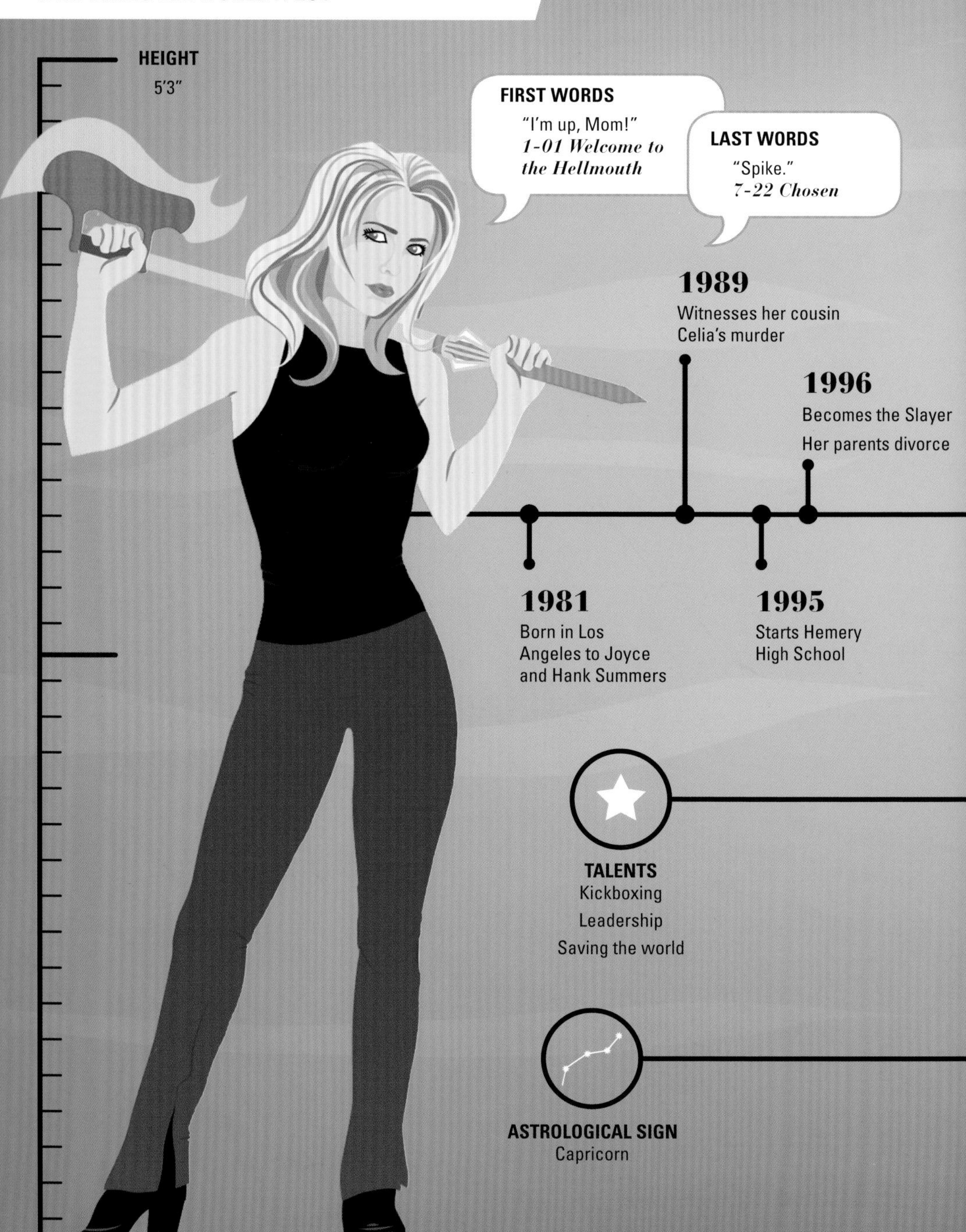

LOVES

Brooding, very old vampires

Mr. Gordo

Boots

HATES

Guns

Letting her friends down

Kathy Newman (her college roommate)

144 (100%) EPISODE COUNT

1997
Starts Sunnydale High
Meets Angel
Dies for the first time during a battle with the Master

1998
Leaves Sunnydale to become a diner waitress in Los Angeles

1999
Enrolls at UC Sunnydale

2000
Starts dating Riley
Dawn arrives

2001
Joyce dies
Dies for the second time by throwing herself into an interdimensional portal
Is brought back to life by Willow
Gets it on with Spike

2003
Leads the potential Slayers into a battle against the Turok-Han vampires

KILL CHART

Category	Count	Percent
VAMPIRES	132	(62.26%)
DEMONS	59.5*	(28.07%)
HUMANS	15	(7.08%)
ROBOTS	4.5*	(2.12%)
SPIRIT BEARS	1	(0.47%)

* When Buffy kills Moloch at the end of *1-08 I, Robot . . . You, Jane*, he is half-demon, half-robot, so each category is awarded 0.5 points.

MAP OF SUNNYDALE

FEATURES

- Founded in 1899 by Richard Wilkins
- Population: 38,500 (1997), 0 (2003)
- 43 churches
- 12 cemeteries (one of them next to a lake)

BEFORE THE SLAYER

THE HISTORY OF SUNNYDALE PRIOR TO BUFFY'S ARRIVAL

[date unknown]

In what will one day be the town of Sunnydale, a portal between this reality and a hell dimension allows demons to pass into our world. ***1-02 The Harvest***

On an unknown date, the portal is closed beneath the Seal of Danzalthar. ***7-16 Storyteller***

Some time after this in a nearby valley, the last pure demon is killed by a Slayer using the M? scythe, which is then embedded in the rock. A pagan temple is founded around the site of the rock. ***7-21 End of Days***

c. 11,000 BC

The Chumash—a Native American people—establish themselves in the area and throughout what will later be called California.

AD 1542

First contact between European settlers and the Chumash.

1770

Spanish settlers arrive in force to claim Chumash territories.

The settlers call the area "Boca del Infierno"—the Hellmouth—suggesting they experience demonic activity. ***1-02 The Harvest***

A monastery is founded on the site of the pagan temple that houses the M? scythe. ***7-21 End of Days***

The old Sunnydale Mission is founded. The Chumash are imprisoned, forced into labor, and herded like animals into missions where they contract diseases such as malaria, smallpox, and syphilis. The few Chumash who rebel are hanged. When a group is accused of stealing cattle, the Spanish kill men, women, and children and cut off ears to show their accusers as proof. ***4-08 Pangs***

1812

A huge earthquake—possibly summoned by the Chumash—buries the old Sunnydale Mission. ***4-08 Pangs***

1824

A wider Chumash uprising takes place in what is now Santa Barbara County.

Late 1800s

Sorcerer Richard Wilkins is living in Sunnydale. Oz finds his photograph more than 100 years later in 1999 and he looks no different. *3-17 Enemies*

According to Faith, Mayor Richard Wilkins "built"—or perhaps founded—Sunnydale for demons to feed on, in exchange for their helping in his ascension. *3-17 Enemies*

c. 1899

The demon Balthazar and his acolytes, El Eliminati, are defeated in the Sunnydale area, probably by Wilkins. A wealthy landowner named Gleaves takes Balthazar's strength-giving amulet, and it is buried with him when he dies. *3-14 Bad Girls*

1903

Wilkins marries Edna May. *3-19 Choices*

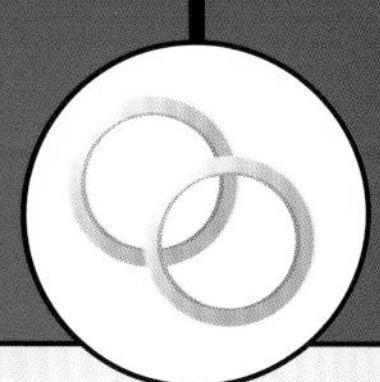

1932

An earthquake swallows the Satanist church at Kingman's Bluff. *6-22 Grave*

1937

Following a rash of murders, the Master tries to open the Hellmouth, but instead unleashes an earthquake that swallows half the town—and him too. *1-02 The Harvest*

1949 to 1960

The Lowell House for Children houses up to 40 adolescents from the area, but director Genevieve Holt imposes a harsh and abusive regime. *4-18 Where the Wild Things Are*

1955

Sunnydale High School is built sometime before this year, with its library located directly above the Hellmouth. James Stanley is a student and Grace Newman a teacher. *2-19 I Only Have Eyes for You*

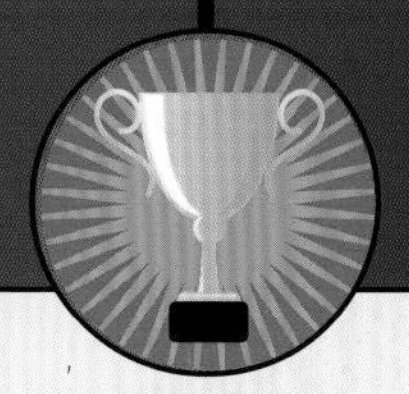

1962

The Lowell House is now part of UC Sunnydale and its students win a trophy. *4-18 Where the Wild Things Are*

c. 1986

Xander and Willow Rosenberg attend kindergarten together and become lifelong friends. *6-22 Grave*

1997

A year after becoming the Slayer, 16-year-old Buffy Summers moves to Sunnydale with her mother, Joyce. Rupert Giles arrives in Sunnydale at roughly the same time, assigned as Buffy's Watcher. *1-01 Welcome to the Hellmouth*

ANATOMY OF A SLAYER

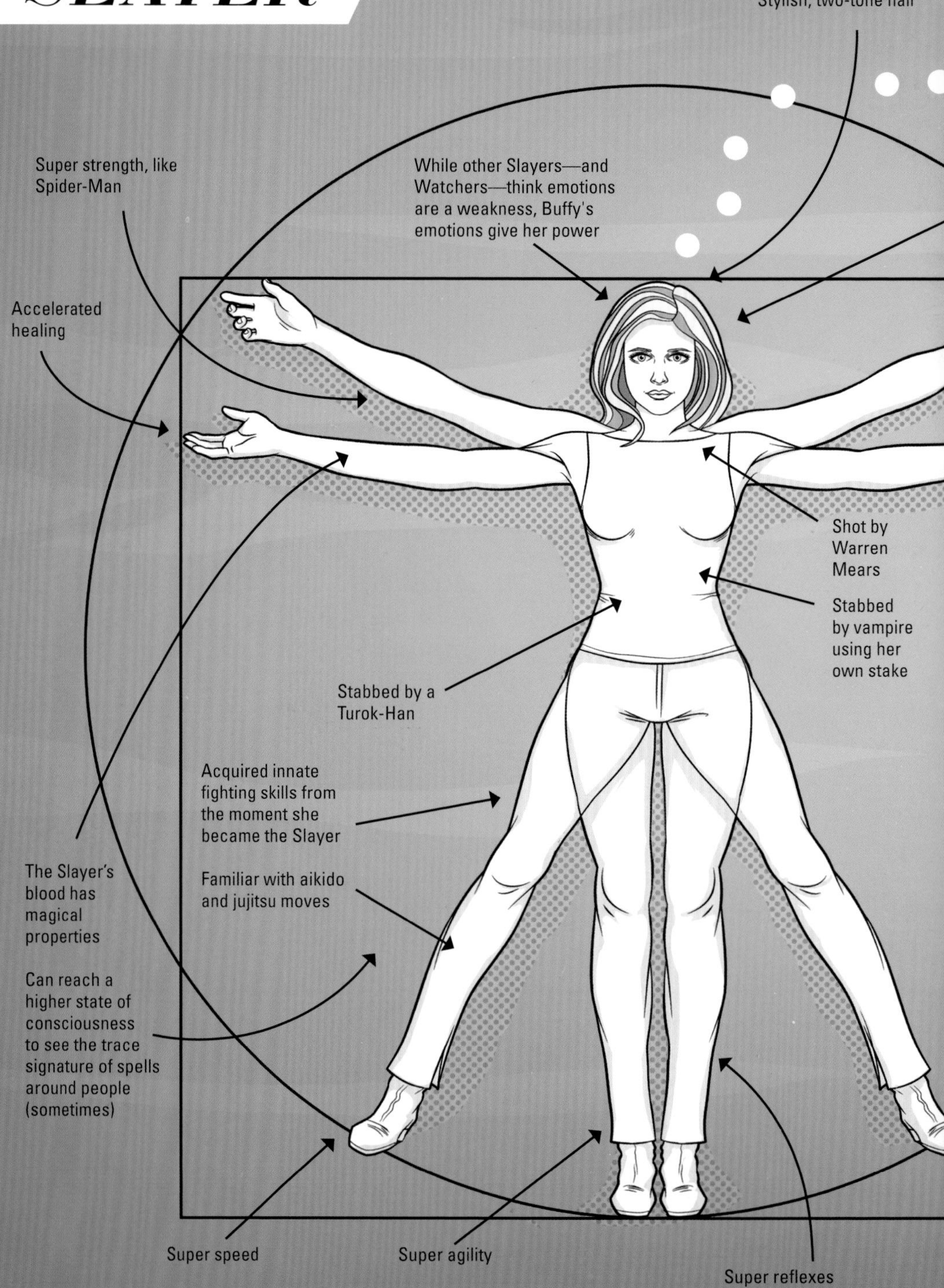

Sometimes dreams of real events to come

WHAT MAKES BUFFY BUFFY?

CORDELIA'S VERDICT

FAITH'S VERDICT

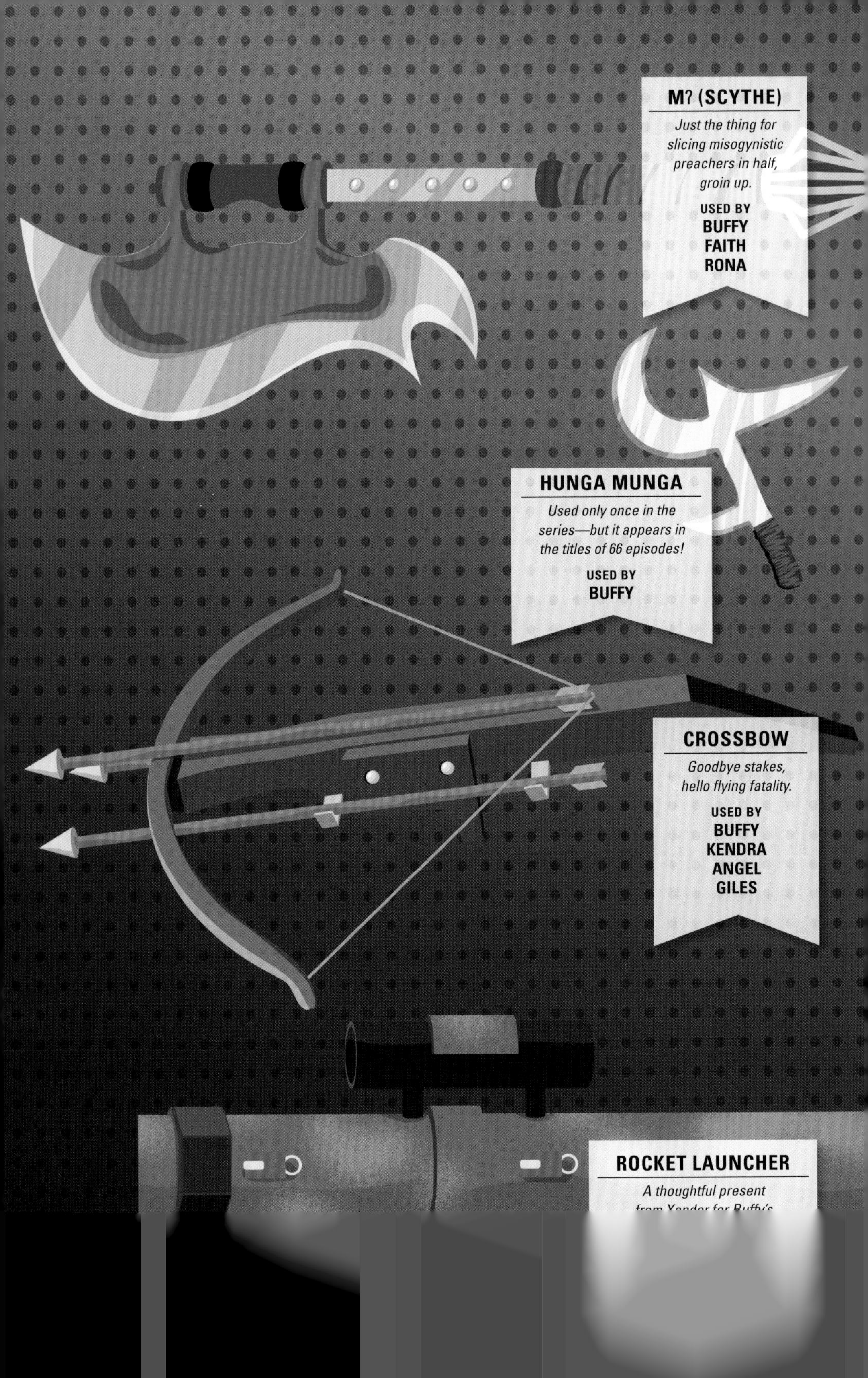

M? (SCYTHE)
Just the thing for slicing misogynistic preachers in half, groin up.
USED BY
BUFFY
FAITH
RONA
HUNGA MUNGA
Used only once in the series—but it appears in the titles of 66 episodes!
USED BY
BUFFY
CROSSBOW
Goodbye stakes, hello flying fatality.
USED BY
BUFFY
KENDRA
ANGEL
GILES
ROCKET LAUNCHER
A thoughtful present

STABBY POINTY THINGS

BUFFY'S MORE THAN JUST A STAKE HOLDER

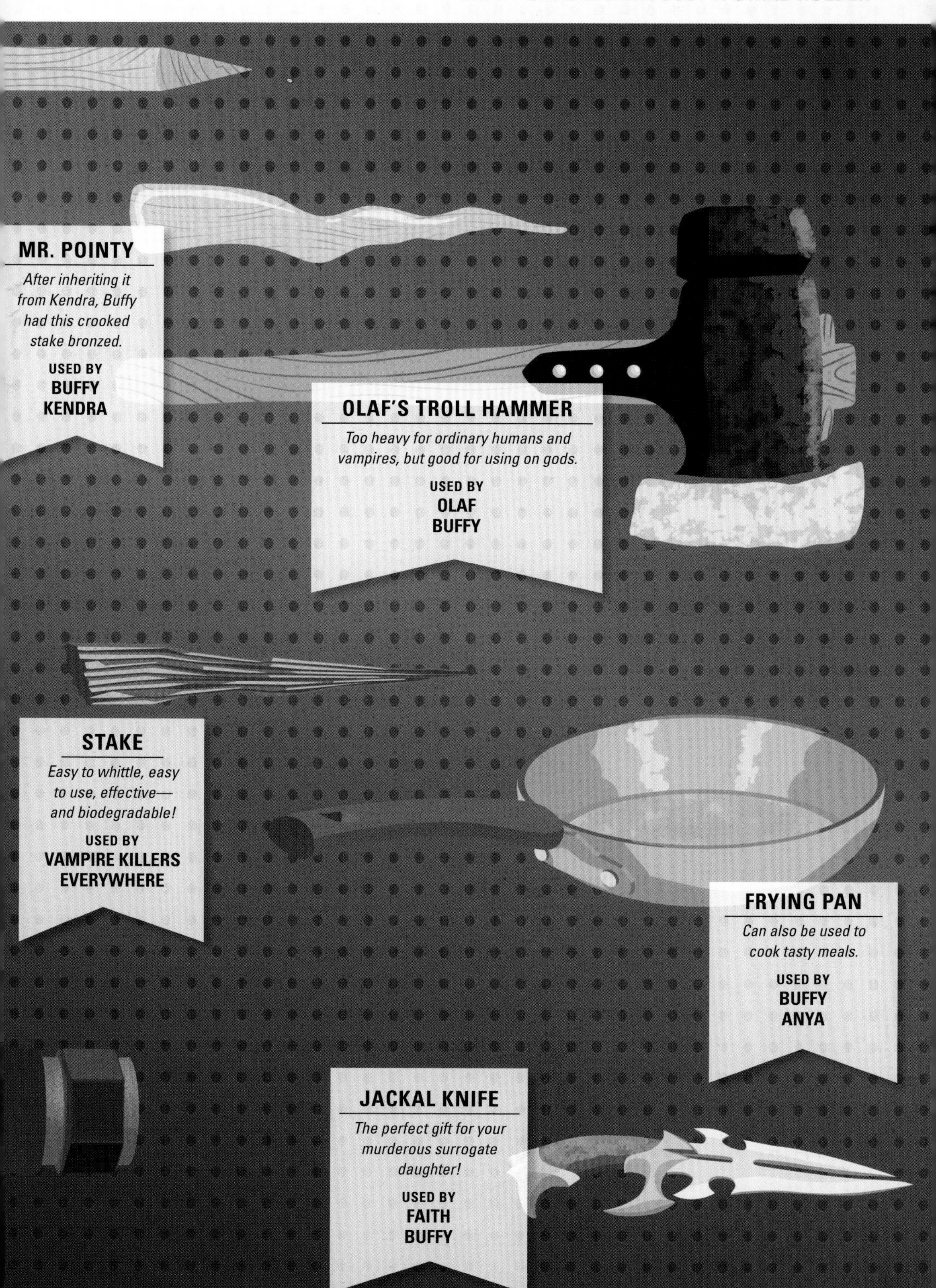

BATTLE OF THE SLAYERS

THERE CAN BE ONLY ONE—EXCEPT FOR THE *OTHER* ONES . . .

ON-SCREEN BATTLES

BUFFY VS **KENDRA YOUNG**

★★

2-09 What's My Line (Part 1)
Kendra sees Buffy smooching Angel and assumes she's a vampire too. Awkward.

★ DRAW ★

ON-SCREEN BATTLES

BUFFY VS **FAITH**

★★★

3-07 Revelations
Faith is told to fight Buffy by her wicked Watcher, Gwendolyn Post.

★ DRAW ★

3-17 Enemies
Faith is angry after being duped by Buffy and Angel.

★ DRAW ★

3-22 Graduation Day (Part 2)
Faith shoots Angel with a poisoned arrow, and Buffy needs Faith's blood to heal him.

★ BUFFY WINS ★

4-15 This Year's Girl
Faith holds Buffy's mom hostage in Buffy's own house.

★ DRAW ★

4-16 Who Are You?
Buffy wants her body back.

★ DRAW ★

OTHER SLAYERS

NAME	FROM	SLAYER DATES	WATCHER	ON-SCREEN KILLS	NO. EPISODES	KILLS PER EPISODE	FIRST APPEARANCE
Kendra Young	Jamaica	1997–1998	Sam Zabuto	1	3	0.33	2-09 What's My Line (Part 1)
Faith	Boston	1998–	Unknown woman; Gwendolyn Post	22	20	1.1	3-03 Faith, Hope & Trick
Sineya	Africa	????	Shadow Men	0 (Kills Xander and Giles in dream.)	3	0	4-22 Restless
Xin Rong	China	????–1900	Bernard Crowley	0	1	0	5-07 Fool for Love
Nikki Wood	New York	????–1977	Unknown	0	2	0	5-07 Fool for Love
Amanda	Sunnydale	2003	None	1	10	0.1	7-04 Help
Kennedy	New York	2003–	None	1	13	0.08	7-10 Bring on the Night
Vi	Unknown	2003–	None	5	8	0.63	7-11 Showtime
Rona	Unknown	2003–	None	1	10	0.1	7-11 Showtime
Chao-Ahn	Shanghai	2003–	None	1	6	0.17	7-14 First Date
Shannon	Unknown	2003–	None	0	3	0	7-18 Dirty Girls

SLAYERS SLAIN

Xin Rong	Killed by Spike
Nikki Wood	Killed by Spike
Kendra Young	Killed by Drusilla
Amanda	Killed by a Turok-Han

BIG BAD LINEUP

WHICH BIG BAD IS BIGGEST?

THE MASTER

APPEARS IN:
Seasons 1–3, 7
9 episodes total

THE ANOINTED ONE

APPEARS IN:
Seasons 1–2
6 episodes total

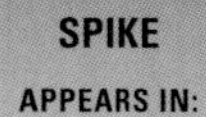

SPIKE

APPEARS IN:
Seasons 2–7
97 episodes total

MAYOR RICHARD WILKINS III (HUMAN FORM)

APPEARS IN:
Seasons 3–4, 7
14 episodes total

THE MAYOR (OLVIKAN FORM)

APPEARS IN:
Season 3
1 episode

8
7
6
5
4
3
2
1
0
DRUSILLA
APPEARS IN:
Seasons 2, 5, 7
7 episodes total
ANGELUS
APPEARS IN:
Seasons 2–3, 5
11 episodes total
ADAM
APPEARS IN:
Seasons 4–7
9 episodes total

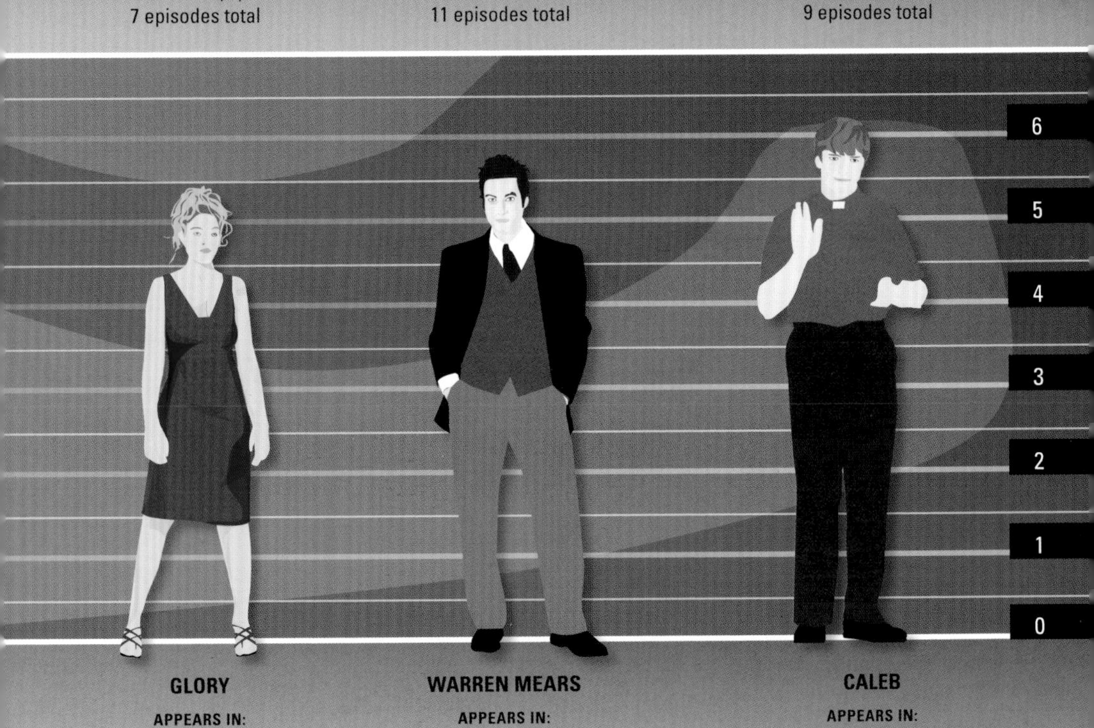
6
5
4
3
2
1
0
GLORY
APPEARS IN:
Seasons 5–7
13 episodes total
WARREN MEARS
APPEARS IN:
Seasons 5–7
16 episodes total
CALEB
APPEARS IN:
Season 7
5 episodes total

BIG BATTLES—THE MASTER

1-12 PROPHECY GIRL

1. The trapped Master hypnotizes Buffy. (32:41)

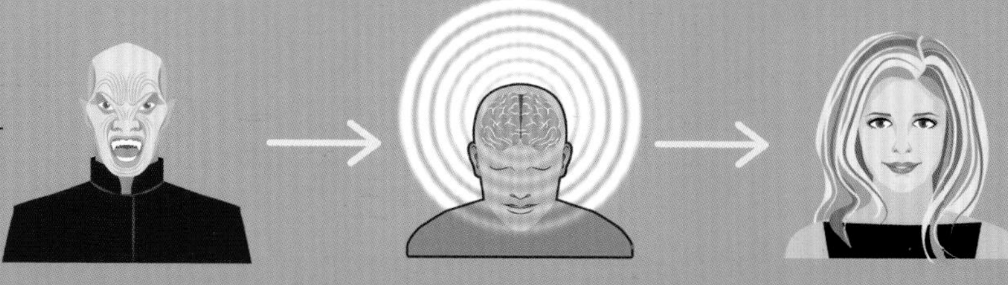

2. The trapped Master kills Buffy—and her blood sets him free. (33:38)

3. Xander saves Buffy using CPR. (35:36)

4. Buffy fights the Master. (40:14)

5. Buffy impales the Master and he turns to dust. (41:04)

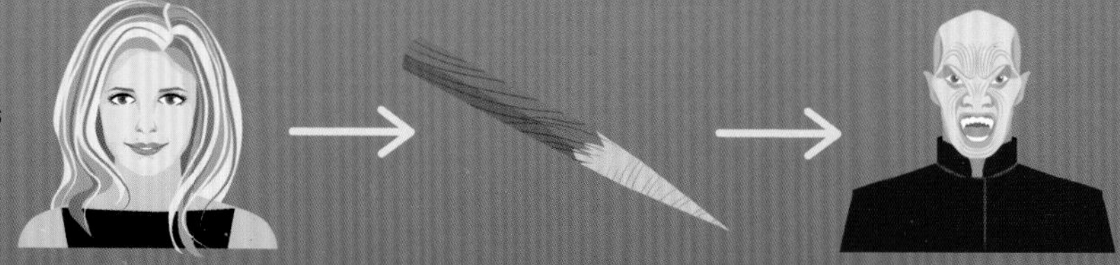

6. Months later, Buffy smashes the Master's skeleton—ensuring he can't return. (38:05 into ***2-01 When She Was Bad***)

KEY DATES

[date unknown]

The Master is sired—all that is known is he's as old as any vampire on record.

1609

The Master sires Darla in Virginia.

1760

The Master meets Angel.

1937

The Master attempts to open the Hellmouth in Sunnydale, but causes an earthquake. A mystical force traps him underground.

1997

The Master finally gains his freedom by killing Buffy, but she recovers and kills him back. Later, she smashes his bones to dust.

But prophecies are tricky creatures. They don't tell you everything. You're the one that sets me free! If you hadn't come, I couldn't go. Think about that!

THE HORROR, THE HORROR

To provoke Buffy, vampires kill Sunnydale students, including friends of Willow and Cordelia

THE HIGH COST OF WINNING

Buffy dies—for a short while

Minor cuts, bruises, and a soggy prom dress

THE HARVEST

And like a plague of boils, the race of man covered the Earth. But on the third day of the newest light would come the Harvest. And the blood of men will flow as wine when the Master will walk among them once more. The Earth will belong to the old ones. And hell itself will come to town.

THE PERGAMUM CODEX

The Master shall rise, and the Slayer [shall die].

WILLOW DANIELLE ROSENBERG

"I AM A SHE-WITCH, A VERY POWERFUL SHE-WITCH—OR WITCH, AS IS MORE ACCURATE. I AM NOT TO BE TRIFLED WITH . . ."
—WILLOW, *7-09 NEVER LEAVE ME*

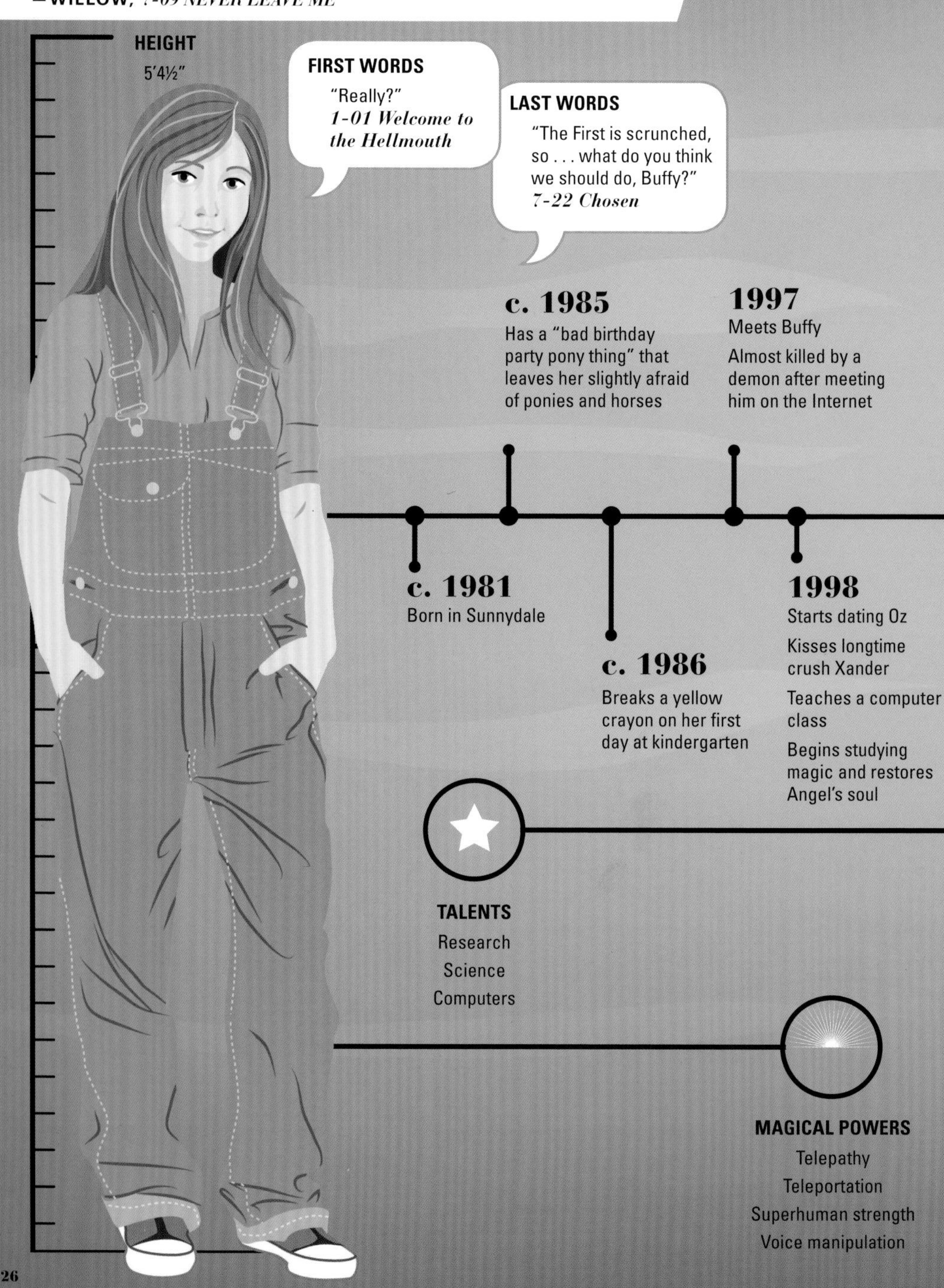

LOVES

A Charlie Brown Christmas

Cats

The "We Hate Cordelia" Club

HATES

Frogs

Spiders

Cordelia

144 (100%) EPISODE COUNT

1999

Willow's mom, under a demon's spell, tries to murder her

Meets her alternate reality doppelgänger

Joins UC Sunnydale

Breaks up with Oz

2000

Falls in love with Tara

2001

Attacks Glory after the hell goddess "brain-sucks" Tara—ouch

2002

Kills Warren after he murders Tara

Tries to destroy the world, is stopped by Xander

2003

Begins a relationship with Kennedy

Performs a spell to infuse every potential Slayer in the world with powers, helping to defeat the First Evil

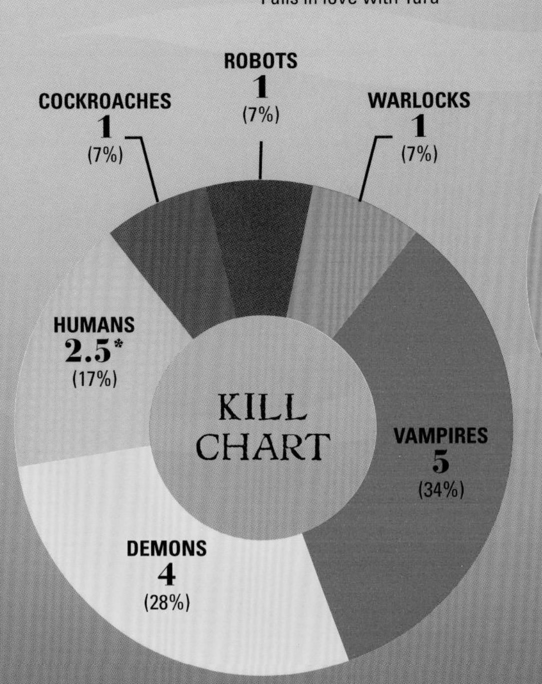

PERSONALITY CHART

KIND 7%

SHY 15%

GEEKY 13%

AWKWARD 10%

BRAVE 55%

*0.5 shared with Xander.

GEEK CHIC

CORDELIA ON THE SCOOBIES' WORST FASHION DISASTERS

A vest top that says, "Hey, I'm a furry ice cream." Dirt-brown, tie- dyed pants that look like her clothes have an infection.

Overall look: "I sleep rough around Venice Beach."

Pink top that matches her vest while at the same time conveying she's not bothered.

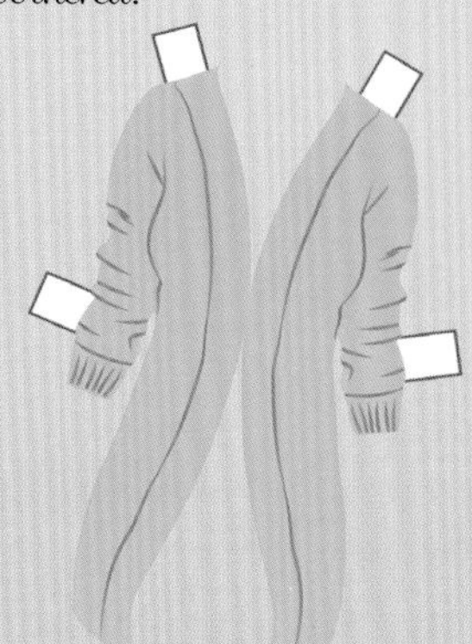

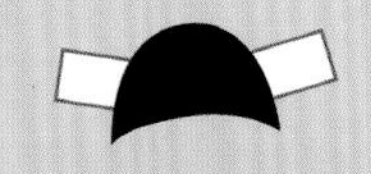

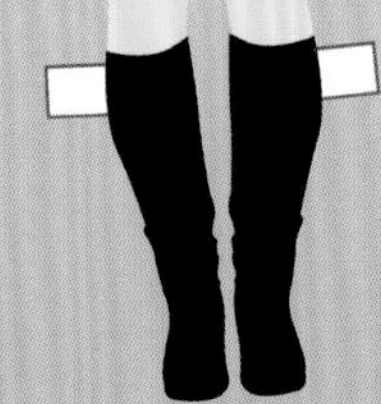

I think the T-shirt's meant to be ironic. Or maybe all of it is.

Sure, you're asked to be a bridesmaid. But given this green travesty, how much do you really like the bride?

BUFFY

I get it. You're busy slaying vampires and whatever. You don't have time to look good. But looking this bad must take special effort, too.

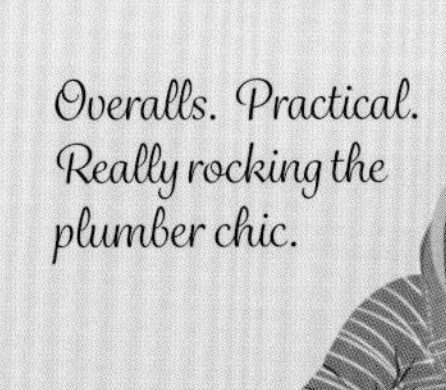

WILLOW

Poor Willow. So clever in some ways like being able to read, but so hopeless with the important things like clothes and boys and did I mention clothes?

Overalls. Practical. Really rocking the plumber chic.

Why can't she just dress like a grown-up?

Trust me—there's no danger of a clothes fluke here.

Don't even get me started on her hats.

Why do all her clothes have such stupid things on them?

Jumper like a hotel carpet.

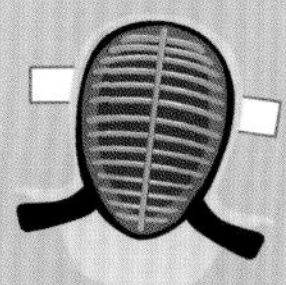

Punch and kick him, and you don't ever have to see his face. What's not to like?

You know, the eye patch suits him.

Short sleeves over long sleeves. Honestly?!

Just one example of his hideous, hideous shirts.

Red pants like rich old people wear.

I'm going to puke. Put it away!

XANDER

This is a carefully cultivated ensemble. It proclaims, "I spent last night asleep in the dump."

Love,
Cordelia

MAGICAL ARTIFACTS

MUST-HAVE ACCESSORIES FOR THE FASHIONABLE SLAYER-ABOUT-TOWN!

THE SCYTHE

WHAT DOES IT DO?	*WHERE WAS IT FOUND?*	*WHAT HAPPENED TO IT?*
Otherwise known as the M?, the Scythe embodies the essence of the Slayer.	In the rock beneath Shadow Valley Vineyards in Sunnydale by Buffy while she was looking for a weapon with which to defeat the First Evil.	Willow used its magical power to make all the Potentials become Slayers simultaneously. Buffy and the Slayers shared the Scythe among them to defeat the Turok-Han.

THE GEM OF AMARA

WHAT DOES IT DO?	*WHERE WAS IT FOUND?*	*WHAT HAPPENED TO IT?*
A mystical ring that grants vampires increased powers and the ability to survive a staking.	Found by Harmony in a tomb in Sunnydale—while her boyfriend, Spike, was searching for it!	Sent by Buffy to Angel in Los Angeles.

AMULET OF BALTHAZAR

WHAT DOES IT DO?	*WHERE WAS IT FOUND?*	*WHAT HAPPENED TO IT?*
It seems that when the demon Balthazar had this amulet taken from him, he lost most of his powers.	In the tomb of a Sunnydale landowner named Gleaves, where it was recovered by Balthazar's minions.	Last seen in the possession of Angel.

INCA SACRED SEAL

WHAT DOES IT DO?	*WHERE WAS IT FOUND?*	*WHAT HAPPENED TO IT?*
Created in the 12th century (approximately) by Inca priests, the Seal prevented sacrificed princesses from waking from their death.	It was never lost—it was on display at a museum in Sunnydale.	Broken by Sunnydale High student Rodney Munson. (D'oh!)

GLOVE OF MYHNEGON

WHAT DOES IT DO?	*WHERE WAS IT FOUND?*	*WHAT HAPPENED TO IT?*
Fires lightning.	In a crypt in Restfield Cemetery, Sunnydale.	Destroyed after Buffy separated it from Gwendolyn Post by cutting off her arm.

ORBS OF NEZZLA'KHAN

WHAT DO THEY DO?	*WHERE WERE THEY FOUND?*	*WHAT HAPPENED TO THEM?*
They give superhuman strength and physical invulnerability to whoever is in possession of them.	In a cave, guarded behind a barrier that only Nezzla demons can pass through—and Jonathan, while wearing a Nezzla skin.	Crushed by Buffy.

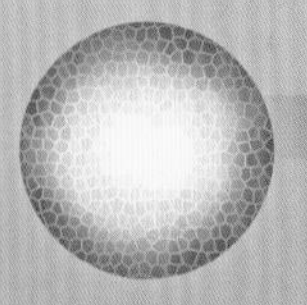

DAGON SPHERE

WHAT DOES IT DO?	*WHERE WAS IT FOUND?*	*WHAT HAPPENED TO IT?*
Protects the person holding it from Glory.	Given to Buffy by a monk of the Order of Dagon.	Crushed to smithereens by Glory.

URN OF OSIRIS

WHAT DOES IT DO?	*WHERE WAS IT FOUND?*	*WHAT HAPPENED TO IT?*
Helps Willow bring Buffy back from the dead.	Being auctioned on eBay by a desert gnome in Cairo.	Shattered by the Hellions road gang.

SHADOW CASTERS

WHAT DO THEY DO?	*WHERE WERE THEY FOUND?*	*WHAT HAPPENED TO THEM?*
Once activated, Shadow Casters will open a portal through time and space.	Originally owned by the first Slayer, they were given to Buffy by Nikki Wood's son, Robin.	Last used by Dawn and Xander.

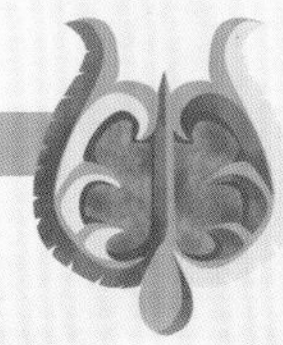

WORD OF VALIOS

WHAT DOES IT DO?	*WHERE WAS IT FOUND?*	*WHAT HAPPENED TO IT?*
Used for completing the Sacrifice of Three.	Bought by Rupert Giles.	Stolen by three Vahrall demons.

SPHERE OF THE FUTURE

WHAT DOES IT DO?	*WHERE WAS IT FOUND?*	*WHAT HAPPENED TO IT?*
Used by the demon Stewart Burns to show false visions of the future to Xander on his wedding day.	Unknown, but perhaps from the hell dimension to which Anyanka banished Stewart in 1914.	Last seen when Stewart used it on Xander.

OVU MOBANI MASK

WHAT DOES IT DO?	*WHERE WAS IT FOUND?*	*WHAT HAPPENED TO IT?*
Causes the dead to become zombies.	Imported from Africa for an art exhibition by Joyce Summers.	Destroyed by Buffy.

PERGAMUM CODEX

WHAT DOES IT DO?	*WHERE WAS IT FOUND?*	*WHAT HAPPENED TO IT?*
An ancient book reputed to contain the most complete prophecies about the Slayer's role in the end years.	Giles thought it was lost in the 15th century, but Angel had a copy and gave it to him.	Last seen after correctly predicting Buffy's death at the hands of the Master.

DARKEST MAGICK

WHAT DOES IT DO?	*WHERE WAS IT FOUND?*	*WHAT HAPPENED TO IT?*
A book of spells and magic so dark it is usually kept off-limits.	Willow took it from the restricted section of the Magic Box.	Possibly absorbed by Willow when she turned dark.

ALEXANDER "XANDER" LAVELLE HARRIS

HIS FRIENDS FIGHT DEMONS AND CAST POWERFUL SPELLS—BUT HE ONCE SAVED THE WORLD WITH LOVE

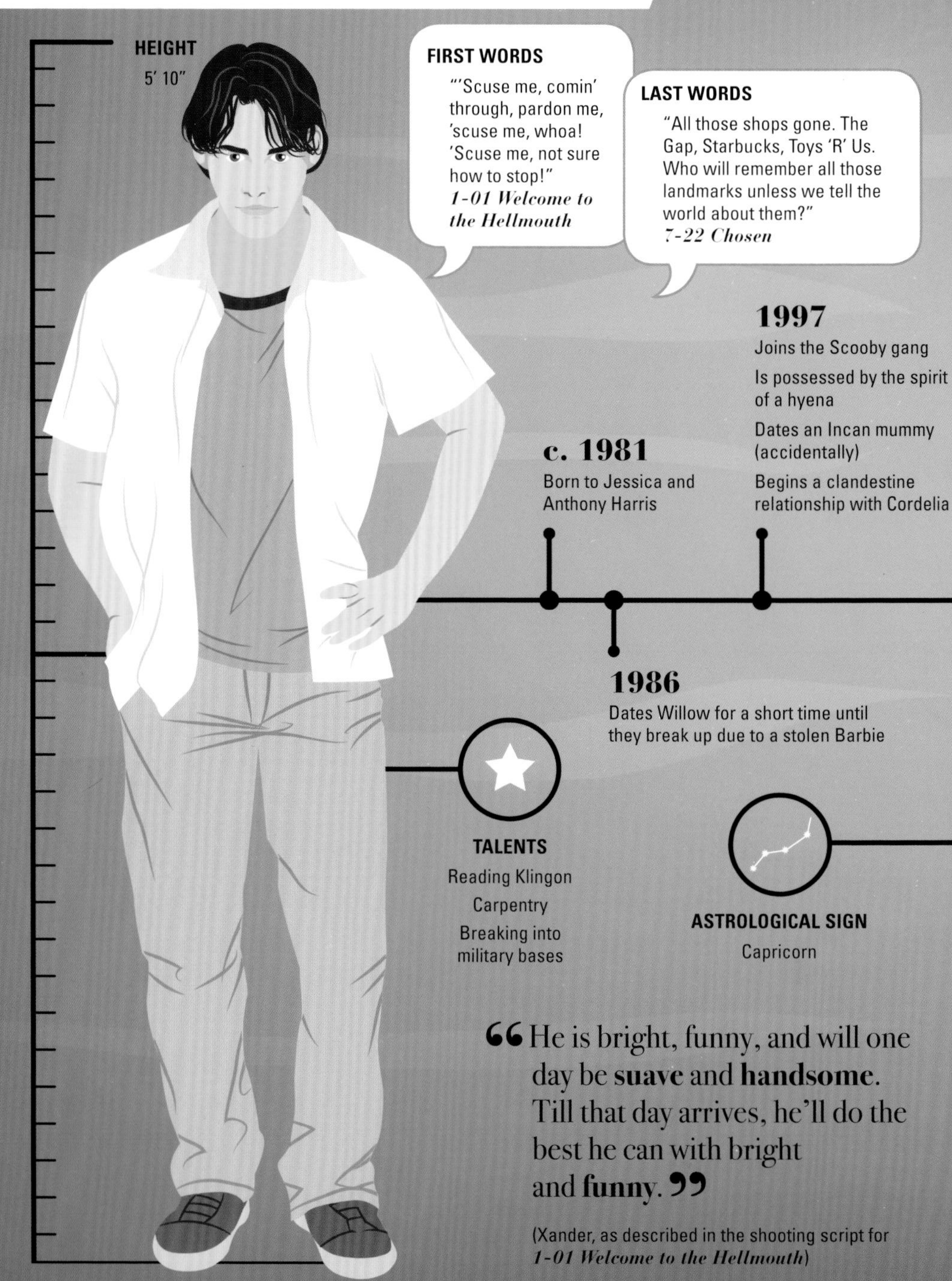

"He is bright, funny, and will one day be **suave** and **handsome**. Till that day arrives, he'll do the best he can with bright and **funny**."

(Xander, as described in the shooting script for *1-01 Welcome to the Hellmouth*)

LOVES
Comic books
Sarcasm
Anya

HATES
Learning
Spike
Clowns

143
(99%)
EPISODE COUNT

1999
Loses his virginity to Faith
Begins dating Anya
Graduates high school and embarks on a cross-country road trip (only getting as far as Oxnard as his car breaks down)
Becomes a construction worker

2001
Asks Anya to marry him

2003
Has his eye gouged out by Caleb

1998
Affair with Cordelia ends

2000
Is split into two by the demon Toth

2002
Leaves Anya at the altar

THE TWO XANDERS (from *5-03 The Replacement*)

Courage	Humor
Confidence	Insecurity

ALSO KNOWN AS
The Zeppo, for being the "useless" part of the Scooby gang (according to Cordelia)

BUTT MONKEY

THE TRIALS AND TRIBULATIONS OF XANDER HARRIS

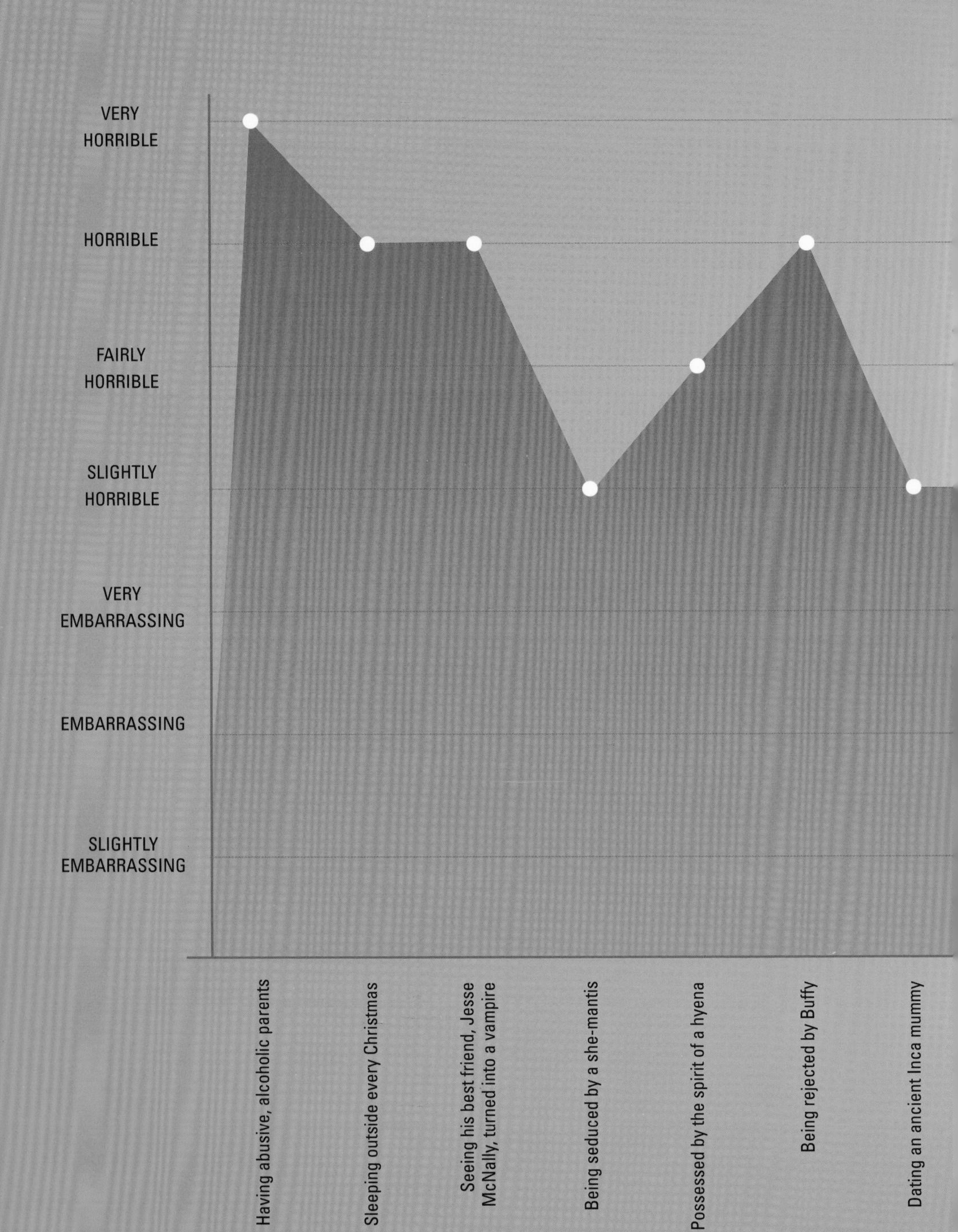

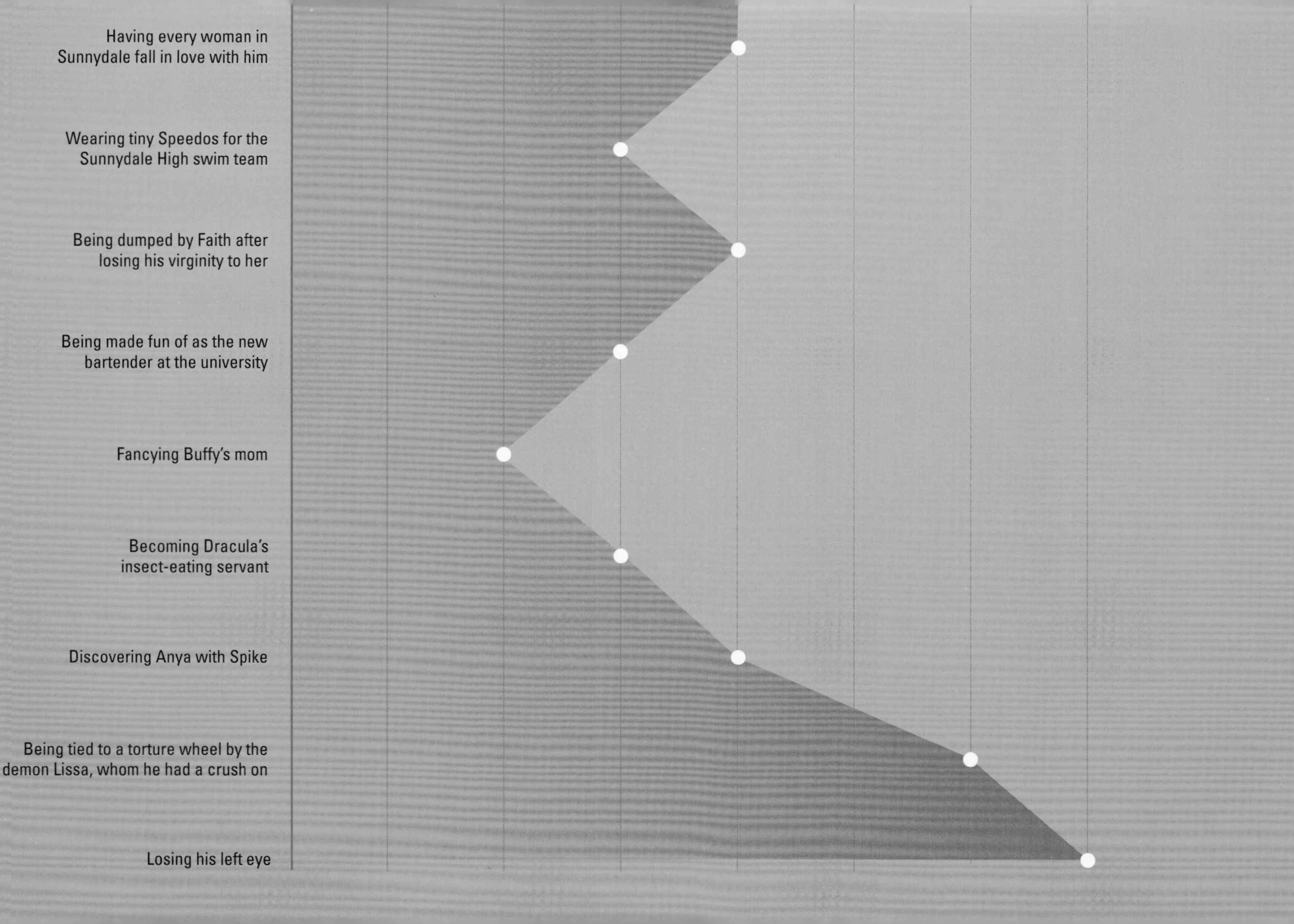

Having every woman in Sunnydale fall in love with him
Wearing tiny Speedos for the Sunnydale High swim team
Being dumped by Faith after losing his virginity to her
Being made fun of as the new bartender at the university
Fancying Buffy's mom
Becoming Dracula's insect-eating servant
Discovering Anya with Spike
Being tied to a torture wheel by the demon Lissa, whom he had a crush on
Losing his left eye

SEEING DOUBLE

"HEY, WAIT TILL YOU HAVE AN EVIL TWIN. SEE HOW *YOU* HANDLE IT!" "I HANDLED IT FINE." —XANDER AND WILLOW, *5-03 THE REPLACEMENT*

Xander

5-03 The Replacement

The demon Toth hits Xander with the Ferula Gemini, which splits him in half, distilling his personality traits into two separate bodies.

The natural state of the two Xanders is to be together, so Willow just has to say, "Let the spell be ended."

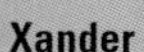

Xander

3-09 The Wish, 3-16 Doppelgangland

Anyanka, the vengeance demon, uses an amulet to grant Cordelia's wish that Buffy never came to Sunnydale, creating an alternative reality where Xander is a vampire.

Buffy kills the vampire Xander before Giles restores reality by destroying the amulet.

Willow

3-09 The Wish, 3-16 Doppelgangland

In the alternate reality created by Anyanka to fulfill Cordelia's wish, Willow also appears as a vampire.

Oz kills the vampire Willow before Giles restores reality by destroying the amulet.

A few weeks later, Anya gets Willow to cast a spell to recover the amulet from the alternate reality—but instead it recovers vampire Willow.

Anya and Willow send vampire Willow back to the alternate reality, just in time to be staked by Oz.

Angel

4-01 The Freshman

Buffy briefly mistakes a random man for Angel.*

Buffybot

5-18 Intervention, 5-22 The Gift, 6-01 Bargaining (Part 1), 6-02 Bargaining (Part 2)

Warren builds a robot version of Buffy for Spike.

The real Buffy dies to save her sister and the world.

The Scoobies use the Buffybot to convince demons that Buffy is still alive and protecting Sunnydale. But they also resurrect Buffy.

The Buffybot is destroyed by the Hellions, a demon road gang.

Warren Mears

6-20 Villains

Warren builds a robot duplicate of himself in his efforts to escape Willow.

Willow destroys the robot duplicate of Warren.

Willow kills Warren.

The First Evil

3-10 Amends, 7-01 Lessons, 7-05 Selfless, 7-07 Conversations With Dead People, 7-08 Sleeper, 7-09 Never Leave Me, 7-10 Bring on the Night, 7-11 Showtime, 7-14 First Date, 7-15 Get It Done, 7-16 Storyteller, 7-18 Dirty Girls, 7-19 Empty Places, 7-20 Touched, 7-21 End of Days, 7-22 Chosen

The First Evil can take the form of anyone dead, and appears as:

Adam (killed by Buffy)

Betty (a victim of Caleb's)

Buffy (killed by the Master and then by herself)

Caleb (killed by Buffy)

Cassie Newton (died of heart failure)

Chloe (killed herself, goaded by the First Evil)

Daniel (killed by Angelus)

Drusilla (sired by Angelus)

Eve (killed by Harbingers of Death)

Glory (killed by Giles)

Jenny Calendar (killed by Angelus)

Jonathan (killed by Andrew)

Joyce (died from a brain aneurysm)

Margaret (killed by Angelus)

The Master (killed by Buffy)

Nikki Wood (killed by Spike)

Richard Wilkins III (killed by Buffy and Giles)

Spike (sired by Drusilla)

Travis (killed by Angelus)

Warren (killed by Willow)

*It's hardly her fault; the random man is played by Angel actor David Boreanaz.

THE WEB

"LOVE'S A FUNNY THING." —SPIKE, *3-08 LOVERS WALK*

Sweet*

Every woman in Sunnydale except Cordelia Chase

Tom Warner

Jesse McNally

Cordelia Chase

Lori

Ampata Gutierrez

RJ Brooks

Mitch Fargo

Wesley Wyndam-Pryce

Kendra Young

XANDER HARRIS

BUFFY SUMMERS

Lissa

Amy Yip

Larry Blaisdell

Natalie French

Julie

Torg

Parker Abrams

Riley Finn

Cameron Walker

Unnamed building manager

Sandy

Scott Hope

Anya Jenkins

Sid the Dummy

Faith Lehane

Olaf the Troll

WILLOW ROSENBERG

Billy Fordham

Veruca

Three unnamed young men

Buffybot

SPIKE

Daniel "Oz" Osbourne

"Malcolm Black" / Moloch

Harmony

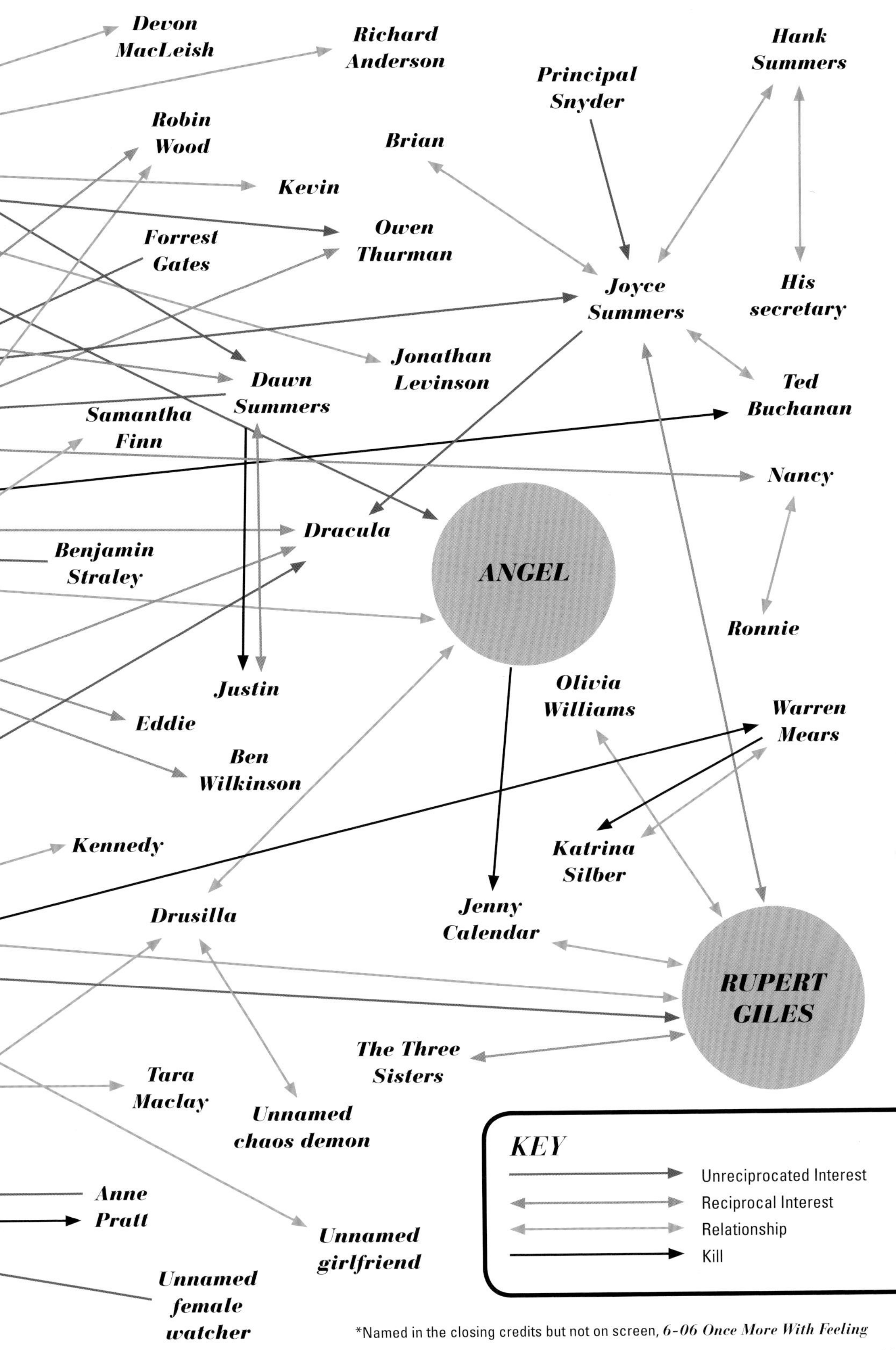

*Named in the closing credits but not on screen, *6-06 Once More With Feeling*

BIG BATTLES—ANGELUS

2-22 BECOMING (PART 2)

1. Angelus draws his own blood, which lets him pull the sword from Acathla, opening a portal to a hell dimension. (29:33)

2. Spike smacks Angelus. (29:58)

3. Buffy fights Angelus. (32:10)

4. Willow's magic restores Angel's soul. (35:07)

5. Buffy kisses Angel. (36:42)

6. To close the portal, Buffy stabs Angel and sends him into the hell dimension. (37:18)

KEY DATES

1753
Darla sires Angel in Galway, Ireland.

1860
Angelus sires Drusilla in London, England.

1898
Angelus is cursed by Romanian gypsies and has his soul returned to him.

1996
Angel meets the demon Whistler in Manhattan.

Angel observes Buffy after she becomes the Slayer while at Hemery High School in Los Angeles.

1997
Angel and Buffy meet.

1998
Angel sleeps with Buffy, and in that moment of pure happiness the curse is lifted and he loses his soul, becoming Angelus once more.

THE HORROR, THE HORROR

Angelus tortures Giles with visions of Jenny Calendar

Buffy's friends are already suffering, with Kendra Young and Jenny dead, and Willow in the hospital with a head injury

THE HIGH COST OF WINNING

Spike betrays Angelus and Drusilla

Buffy banishes Angel—even though he has his soul back—to the hell dimension

Buffy leaves Sunnydale

He will swallow the world.

And every creature living on this planet will go to hell.

RUPERT GILES

"A SLAYER SLAYS, A WATCHER . . ."

—GILES, ***1-01 WELCOME TO THE HELLMOUTH***

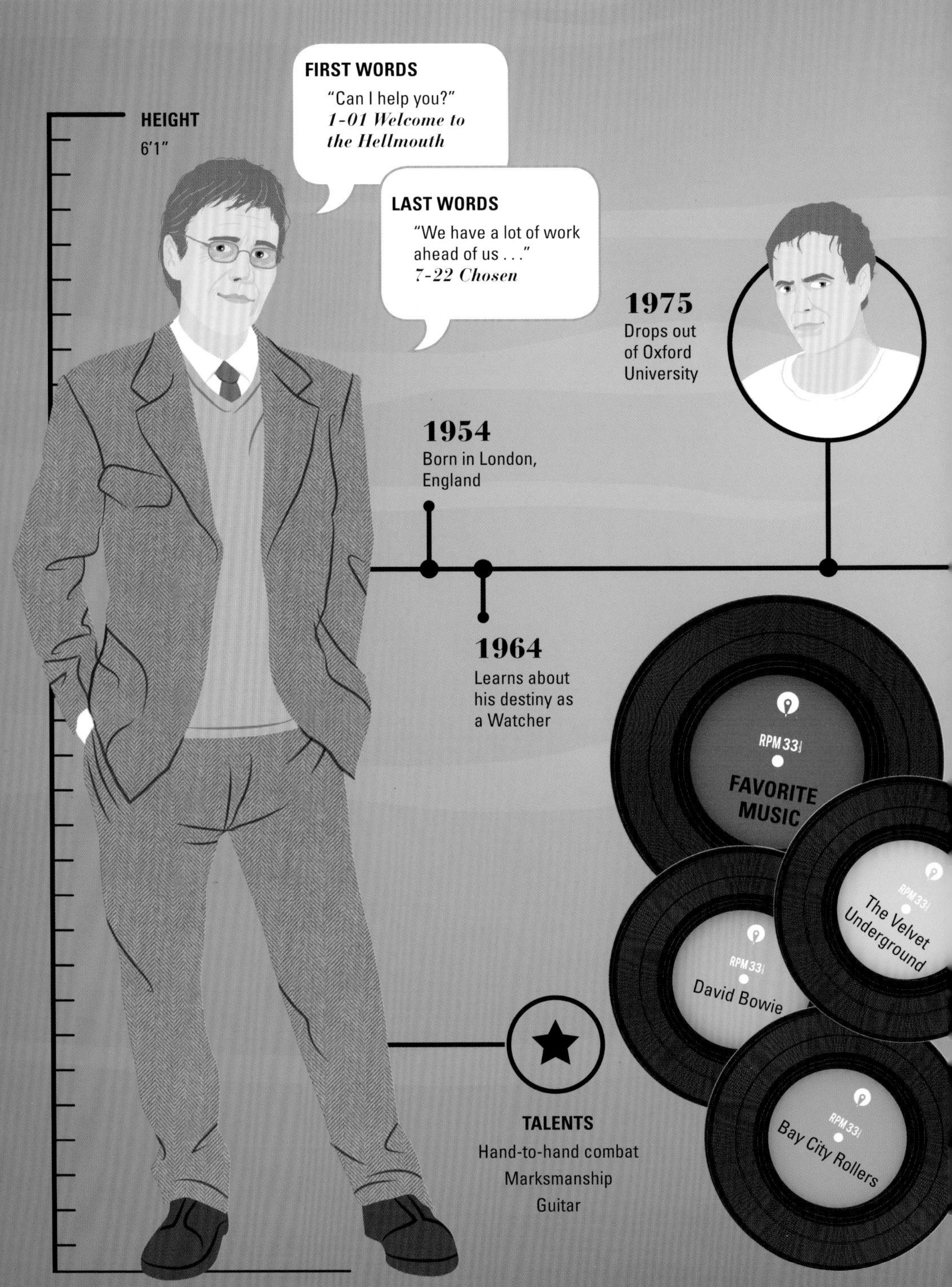

LOVES
Books
Tea
Halloween

HATES
Technology
Pop music
The modern world

121 (84%)
EPISODE COUNT

100%
Percentage of episodes featuring Giles in which he wipes his glasses

1980
Accepts his future as a Watcher

1990s
Moves to Sunnydale

1997
Becomes Watcher to Buffy Summers

Starts dating Sunnydale High teacher Jenny Calendar

1999
Is fired as Buffy's Watcher and replaced by Wesley Wyndam-Pryce

Begins a relationship with old flame Olivia Williams

2000
Is turned into a Fyarl demon by Ethan Rayne's spell

Becomes Buffy's Watcher again

2001
Moves back to England after Buffy's death

2002
Returns to Sunnydale

NICKNAMES
Snobby
Crusty Old Alfred
Captain Slowpoke
Rupy
Ripper

GILES'S ENGLISH HOMES
Westbury
London

I'M ONLY SLEEPING

ALL THE TIMES GILES IS KNOCKED UNCONSCIOUS

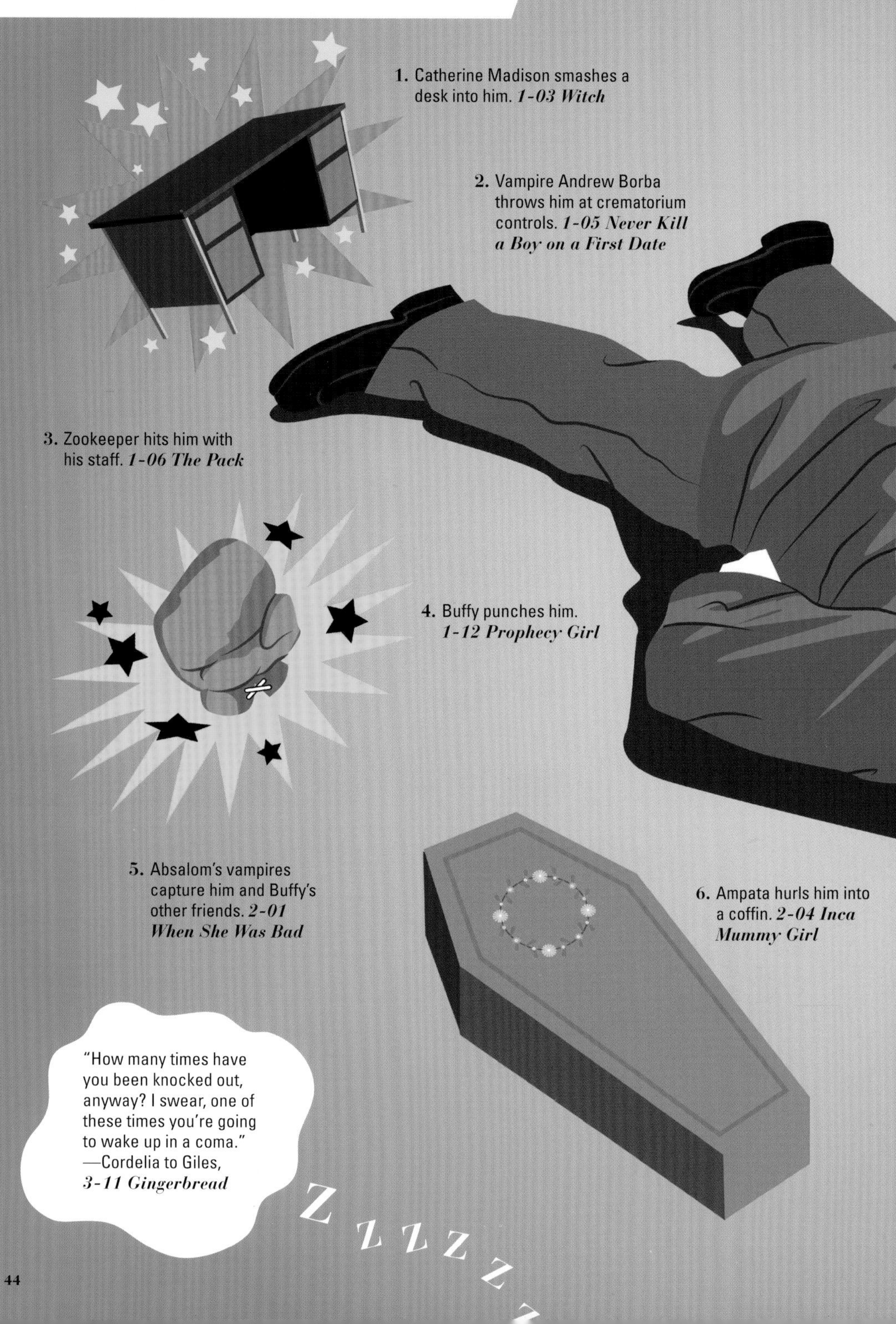

1. Catherine Madison smashes a desk into him. *1-03 Witch*

2. Vampire Andrew Borba throws him at crematorium controls. *1-05 Never Kill a Boy on a First Date*

3. Zookeeper hits him with his staff. *1-06 The Pack*

4. Buffy punches him. *1-12 Prophecy Girl*

5. Absalom's vampires capture him and Buffy's other friends. *2-01 When She Was Bad*

6. Ampata hurls him into a coffin. *2-04 Inca Mummy Girl*

"How many times have you been knocked out, anyway? I swear, one of these times you're going to wake up in a coma."
—Cordelia to Giles,
3-11 Gingerbread

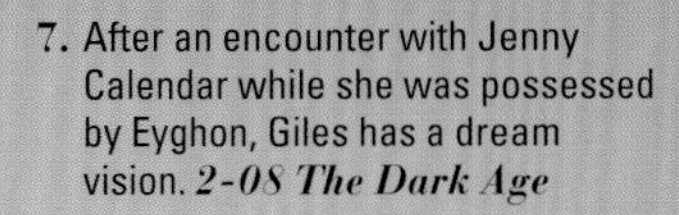

7. After an encounter with Jenny Calendar while she was possessed by Eyghon, Giles has a dream vision. *2-08 The Dark Age*

8. Giles and the others are unconscious after the Bezoar is killed. *2-12 Bad Eggs*

9. Angelus hits him. *2-17 Passion*

10. Drusilla's gang of vampires beat him up. *2-21 Becoming (Part 1)*

11. Buffy shoots him with a tranquillizer gun. *3-04 Beauty and the Beasts*

12. Vampires Candy and Lyle Gorch knock him out. *3-05 Homecoming*

13. Rogue Watcher Gwendolyn Post hits him. *3-07 Revelations*

14. Drugged by Mothers Opposed to the Occult. *3-11 Gingerbread*

15. Ethan Rayne spikes his drink. *4-12 A New Man*

16. M'Fashnik demon hits him. *6-04 Flooded*

17. He and the others are knocked out by Willow's spell. *6-08 Tabula Rasa*

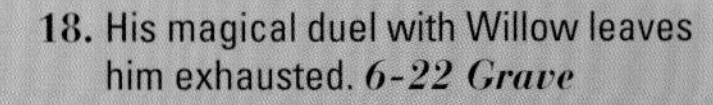

18. His magical duel with Willow leaves him exhausted. *6-22 Grave*

GILES'S SCOOBY REPORTS

FOUND IN THE RUINS OF THE HEADQUARTERS OF THE WATCHERS' COUNCIL OF BRITAIN AFTER THE 2002 EXPLOSION

Dear Quentin,

Please find enclosed assessments of the Slayer and her entourage as requested. As always, I'd welcome any comments or insight you might have.

Rupert

Name: BUFFY SUMMERS

Subject	Comment	Mark
Fighting	Impressive. Buffy shows commendable aptitude and commitment in learning new vampire slaying techniques. Well done.	**A+**
Attitude	Buffy would do better at her job if she wasn't constantly distracted by boys (particularly those of the vampiric variety). Ahem.	**B**
General comments	Buffy is an able Slayer, but has a somewhat trying tendency to not take the job seriously. As I've said many, many times, due to her naturally rebellious nature, some flexibility is required in training her.	

SUNNYDALE HIGH

Name: WILLOW ROSENBERG

Subject	Comment	Mark
Fighting	Poor. Willow is, not to put too fine a point on it, hardly cut out for physical conflict.	**D**
Attitude	Willow shows great enthusiasm and a willingness to learn more about the perils facing our world. She is an efficient researcher and her growing interest in magic is very encouraging. She does, however, put a little too much faith in this "Internet."	**A+**
General comments	Willow is a resourceful, loyal, and admirably inquisitive member of the "Scooby Gang," as they are inclined to call themselves.	

SUNNYDALE HIGH

Name: XANDER HARRIS

Subject	Comment	Mark
Fighting	Xander has great strength and is an invaluable aid to Buffy in her nighttime patrol at the cemetery. Impressive staking techniques to boot.	**B+**
Attitude	Though Xander shows commitment in the fight against vampires and demons, his need to always play the class clown does him no favors. I do believe that if Xander could listen more and quip a bit less, it might stand him in good stead.	**C+**
General comments	Xander's bothersome tendency to see every important meeting as an opportunity to joke around masks, I fear, a deep insecurity. He should trust that his friends like and respect him.	

SUNNYDALE HIGH

Name: CORDELIA CHASE

Subject	Comment	Mark
Fighting	Not one of Cordelia's strong points, lest she breaks a nail or scuffs her highly impractical shoes.	**D**
Attitude	Cordelia seems terribly uninterested in the various threats to Sunnydale, only seeming to care when the danger threatens a planned shopping trip.	**D-**
General comments	I'm not even sure why we invite her to our meetings . . . I can't imagine any of the Council members would find much to admire in her.	

SUNNYDALE HIGH

Name: DANIEL "OZ" OSBOURNE

Subject	Comment	Mark
Fighting	Oz's nocturnal activities as a werewolf mean that some nights we're tied up trying to save people from him!	**D**
Attitude	Oz, I must say, has a laid-back attitude to most things, and his relaxed stoicism can be a welcome tonic to his friends' occasional hysteria.	**B**
General comments	Oz is a valued member of the Scooby Gang, someone whose wisdom belies his years. He makes some bloody awful music, though.	

GLOSSARY OF BUFFY-ISMS

WATCHER'S DIARY —RUPERT GILES

TOP SECRET
By order of the Watchers' Council of Great Britain

Entry #1, 10 March 1997

Slayer is willful and insolent. Her abuse of the English language is such that I understand only every other sentence . . .

bad (adj.)

1. Unpleasant or unwelcome.
2. Good. *(noun)*
3. A mistake ("My bad" = "I apologize for my error").

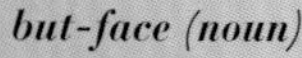

but-face (noun)

What Giles looks like when he's about to say "but."

cookie (noun)

1. Biscuit.
2. Buffy when she's ready to date again.

dust (verb)

To successfully eliminate a vampire.

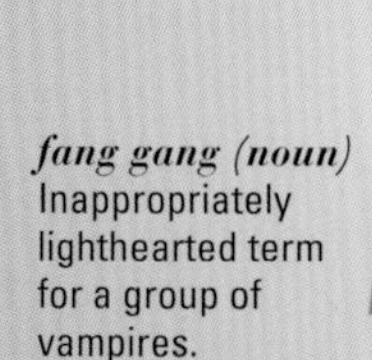

fang gang (noun)

Inappropriately lighthearted term for a group of vampires.

five by five (noun)

1. A good, clear signal in radio communications. *(adj.)*
2. As used by Faith: good.

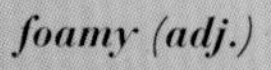

foamy (adj.)

Descriptive of beer, especially magically affected beer.

jones (verb)

To desire.

great googly moogly (interjection)

Expression of surprise, such as when your best friend telepathically speaks to you without warning.

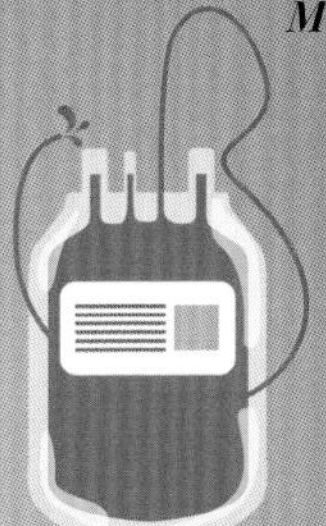

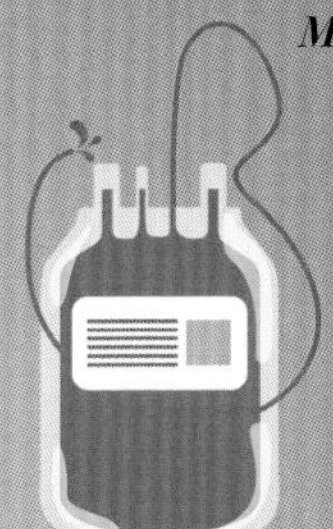

McPlasma (noun)

Blood that has not come directly from a human body.

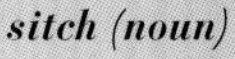

sitch (noun)

Situation. Usually when something's gone wrong.

Princess Margaret

A nickname for Wesley Wyndam-Pryce.

über-suck, the (noun)

Extremely bad, e.g. a student exchange program with a murderous Incan mummy.

smellementary (adj.)

Used to describe a straightforward olfactory deduction.

vamp (noun)

Vampire (casual).

wacky, the (noun)

Irrational behavior when in love.

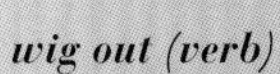

wig out (verb)

To become excitable or wild.

WELCOME TO THE HELLMOUTH

SCHOOL'S OUT FOR SUMMERS

Energy emanating from the Hellmouth causes strange phenomena in the vicinity

Old Sunnydale High (blown up in 1999)

Room directly below school library, with Hellmouth like a crack in the floor

Long chasm through rock

Hell dimension

Three-headed, tentacled demon—seemingly killed in *3-13 The Zeppo*

OPEN AND SHUT

1997 The Master succeeds in opening the Hellmouth, but it is closed again when Buffy kills him. *1-12 Prophecy Girl*

1999 The Sisterhood of Jhe succeed in opening the Hellmouth but Buffy and her friends close it again. *3-13 The Zeppo*

2000 Buffy dives into the Hellmouth to retrieve the last of three Vahrall demons, whose self-sacrifice would have opened the portal again. *4-11 Doomed*

"Even after the Hellmouth was closed, you could still hear it screaming." —Willow, *3-13 The Zeppo*

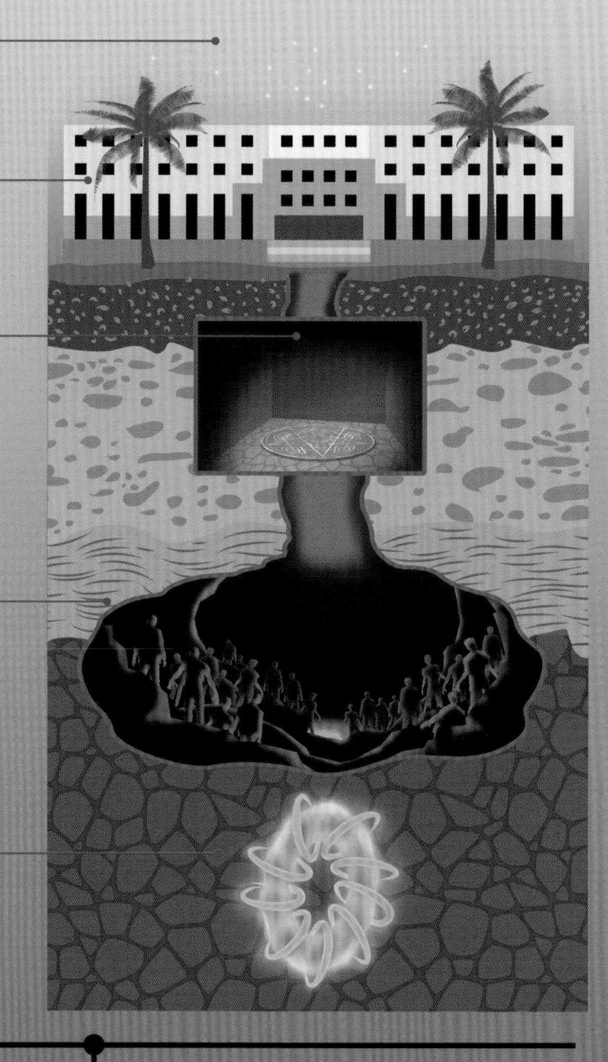

2002

The First Evil convinces Andrew to kill his friend Jonathan so that he bleeds on the Seal of Danzalthar to open the Hellmouth. We later learn Jonathan didn't contain enough blood. *7-07 Conversations with Dead People*

The First Evil cuts Spike so that he bleeds on the Seal of Danzalthar and opens it. *7-09 Never Leave Me*

Having released a Turok-Han vampire, the seal closes again. *7-10 Bring on the Night*

2003

The demon Lissa bleeds Xander to reopen the seal; Principal Wood rescues Xander and the seal closes, chopping off the arm of an emerging Turok-Han. *7-14 First Date*

Possessed students bleed on the seal, but before it can be fully opened, Andrew's tears close it. *7-16 Storyteller*

Buffy, Faith, and the potential Slayers cut themselves to open the seal and face the hundreds of Turok-Han vampires beneath. Spike destroys the vampires and the Hellmouth . . . but Giles says there's another Hellmouth in Cleveland. *7-22 Chosen*

Note: For a history of the Hellmouth before Buffy arrived in Sunnydale, see page **14**.

CLASS OF '99

THE NAMED MEMBERS OF BUFFY'S YEAR AT SUNNYDALE HIGH—AND WHAT BECAME OF THEM

◎ HEIDI BARRIE
fate unknown after **1-06 The Pack**

~~LARRY BLAISDELL~~
dies in **3-22 Graduation Day (Part 2)**

◎ MICHELLE BLAKE
fate unknown after **3-05 Homecoming**

★ LANCE BROOKS
survives, seen in **7-06 Him**

◎ LISA CAMPITI
fate unknown after **1-09 The Puppet Show**

◎ HOLLY CHARLESTON
fate unknown after **3-05 Homecoming**

★ CORDELIA CHASE
survives high school, moves to Los Angeles after **3-22 Graduation Day (Part 2)**

~~PETER CLARNER~~
killed by Angel in **3-04 Beauty and the Beasts**

◎ LISHANNE DAVIS
fate unknown after **1-03 Witch**

◎ KYLE DUFOURS
fate unknown after **1-06 The Pack**

◎ LAURA EGLER
fate unknown after **1-10 Nightmares**

~~ANYA EMERSON~~
survives high school to die in **7-22 Chosen**

◎ CHRIS EPPS
fate unknown after **2-02 Some Assembly Required**

◎ MITCH FARGO
fate unknown after **1-11 Out of Mind, Out of Sight**

~~DEBBIE FOLEY~~
killed by Peter Clarner in **3-04 Beauty and the Beasts**

◎ ERIC GITTLESON
fate unknown after **2-02 Some Assembly Required**

◎ AMBER GROVE
suffered burns in **1-03 Witch**, but fate after that unknown

~~AMPATA GUTIERREZ~~
dies in **2-04 Inca Mummy Girl**

★ ALEXANDER HARRIS
survives

◎ TOR HAUER
fate unknown after **1-06 The Pack**

◎ SCOTT HOPE
survives high school, fate unknown after **7-07 Conversations with Dead People**

◎ FREDERICK IVERSON
fate unknown after **3-18 Earshot**

◎ RHONDA KELLEY
fate unknown after **1-06 The Pack**

★ HARMONY KENDALL
becomes a vampire in **3-22 Graduation Day (Part 2)**, but survives

~~DAVE KIRBY~~
dies in **1-08 I, Robot . . . You, Jane**

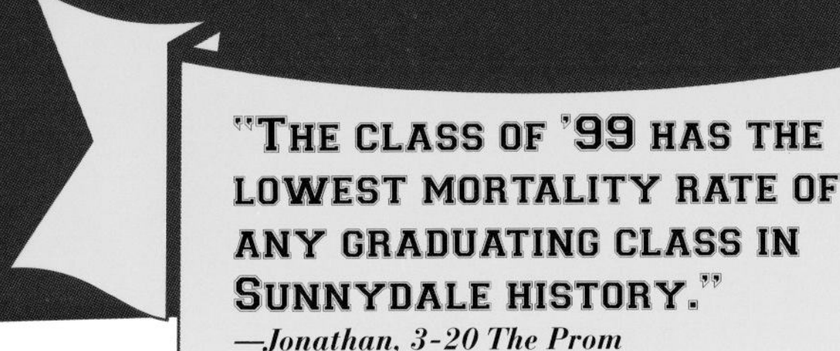

~~JONATHAN LEVINSON~~
survives high school, dies in 7-07 **Conversations with Dead People**

LANCE LINCOLN
fate unknown after 1-06 **The Pack**

DEVON MACLEISH
survives high school, fate unknown after 4-19 **New Moon Rising**

AMY MADISON
turned into a rat in 3-11 **Gingerbread**, permanently turned back into a human in 6-09 **Smashed**, fate unknown after 7-13 **The Killer in Me**

BLAYNE MOLL
fate unknown after 1-04 **Teacher's Pet**

HOGAN MARTIN
fate unknown after 3-18 **Earshot**

JACK MAYHEW
fate unknown after 3-20 **The Prom**

DANIEL OSBOURNE*
becomes a werewolf, survives high school, fate unknown after 4-19 **New Moon Rising**

WILLOW ROSENBERG
survives

~~FRITZ SIEGEL~~
dies in 1-08 **I, Robot . . . You, Jane**

BUFFY ANNE SUMMERS
dies in 1-12 **Prophecy Girl**, recovers, survives high school

BEN STRALEY
fate unknown after 2-19 **I Only Have Eyes for You**

OWEN THURMAN
fate unknown after 1-05 **Never Kill a Boy on the First Date**

LYSETTE TORCHIO
fate unknown after 3-13 **The Zeppo**

~~HOLDEN WEBSTER~~
survives high school, does an internship at Sunnydale Mental Hospital, is sired by Spike and dusted by Buffy in 7-07 **Conversations with Dead People**

PERCY WEST
survives high school, fate unknown after 4-11 **Doomed**

TUCKER WELLS
fate unknown after 3-20 **The Prom**, but his brother Andrew mentions him in 7-22 **Chosen**.

JASON WHEELER
has apparently been in the chronic ward of Sunnydale Mental Hospital since graduation (7-07 **Conversations with Dead People**)

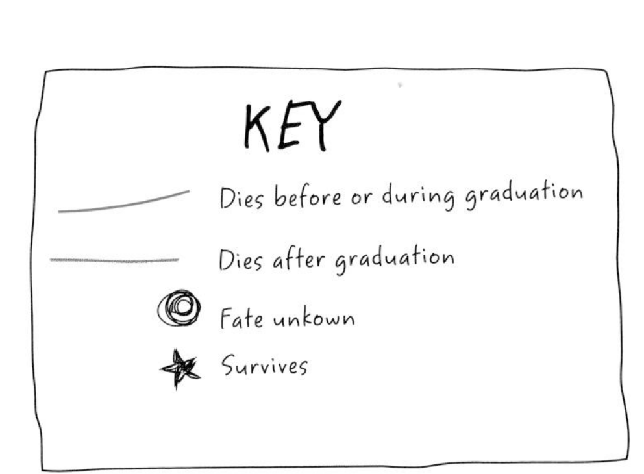

* Oz is a year older than Buffy and her friends, but he had to repeat his senior year so graduated with the class of '99.

BIG BATTLES—GRADUATION DAY

3-22 GRADUATION DAY (PART 2)

1. Buffy stabs Faith with the dagger she received from Mayor Wilkins. (41:00—in *3-21 Graduation Day, Part 1*)

2. Buffy shares a dream with Faith in which they make up. (15:16)

3. Mayor Wilkins ascends, becoming a pure demon, the embodiment of Olvikan. (31:03)

4. Buffy taunts Mayor Wilkins with the dagger she used to stab Faith. (35:39)

5. The mayor chases Buffy. (35:57)

6. Buffy lures the mayor into a library full of explosives. (36:36)

KEY DATES

[date unknown]
The demon Olvikan dies and is buried in a volcanic eruption on Kauai.

c. 1199
A sorcerer achieves ascension in the Koskov Valley in the Urals and becomes the embodiment of the demon Lohesh, the four-winged soul-killer.

c. 1997*
Professor of volcanology Lester Worth from Sunnydale uncovers the remains of Olvikan on Kauai.

1999
Worth is murdered by Faith because the mayor hopes to hide the fact that an ascended demon can die.

*We're not told when Worth conducted his work, but it seems likely it was quite recent—otherwise why wouldn't Wilkins have had him murdered sooner?

THE HORROR, THE HORROR

Buffy and Faith suffer several injuries as a result of their fight

Mayor Wilkins suffocates the prone Buffy in the hospital

THE HIGH COST OF WINNING

Many at the graduation ceremony die—including Larry Blaisdell and Principal Snyder

Harmony Kendall is sired

Wesley Wyndam-Pryce is hospitalised

Sunnydale High School is destroyed

ANGEL

"DON'T WORRY, I DON'T BITE!"

—ANGEL, *1-01 WELCOME TO THE HELLMOUTH*

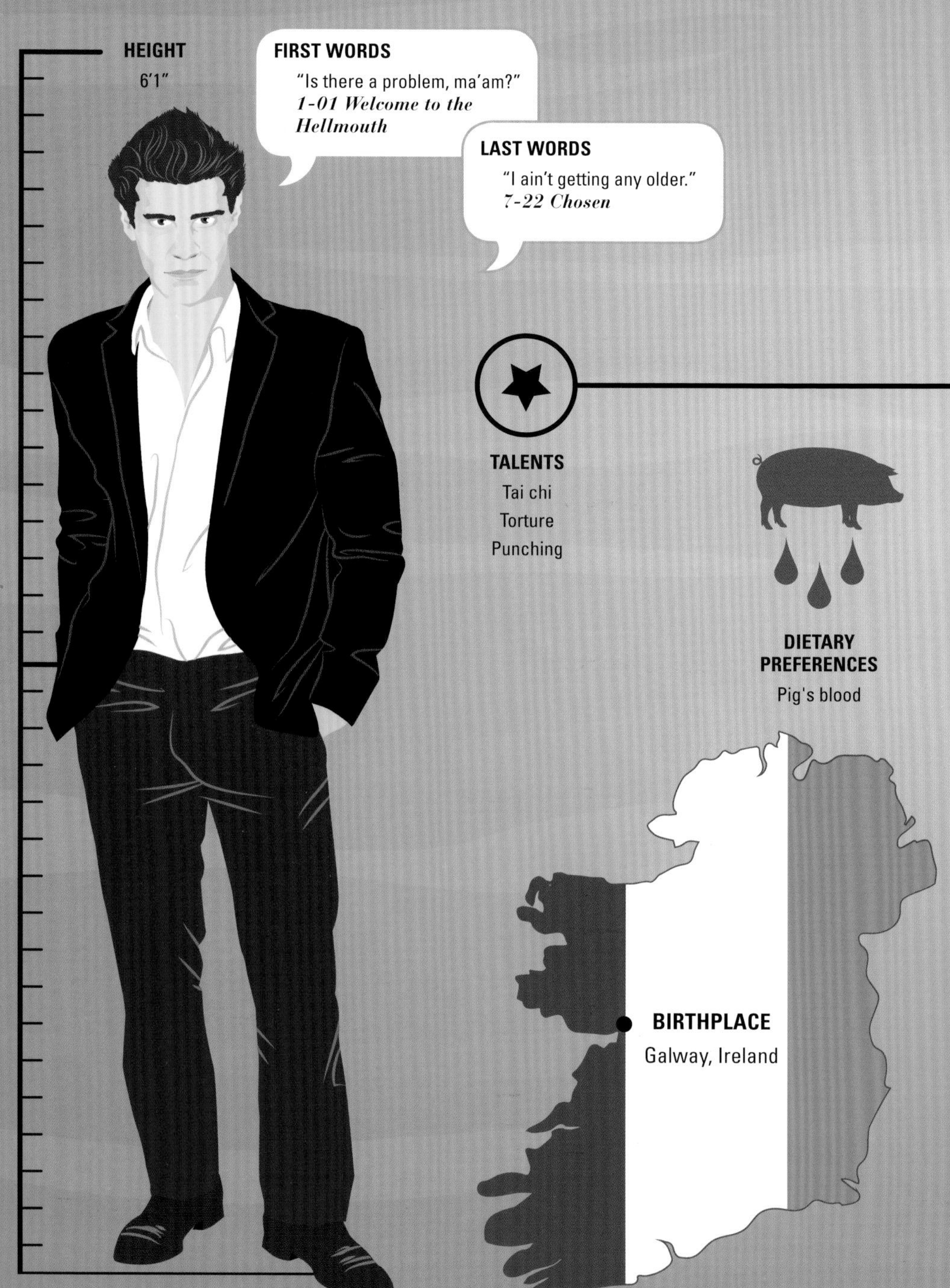

LOVES
The color black
Barry Manilow
Sartre

HATES
Dancing
Smiling
Spike

58
(40%)
EPISODE COUNT

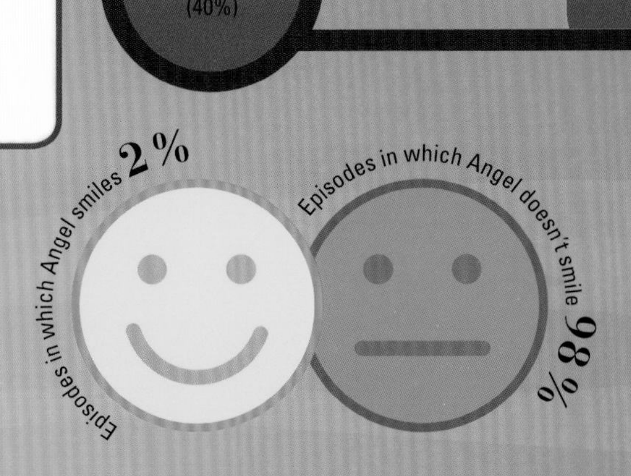

ANGEL'S GIFT TO BUFFY FOR HER

17th
BIRTHDAY
A Claddagh ring

"Wear it with the heart pointing towards you. It means you belong to somebody. Like this. Put it on." ***2-13 Surprise***

TATTOO
A griffin from the Book of Kells, with the letter *A* beneath it

ALTER EGOS
Liam (real name)
Angelus
The Scourge of Europe

ALSO KNOWN AS

1. Captain Forehead (by Spike)
2. Broody Boy (by Cordelia)
3. Angry Puppy (by Buffy)
4. King of Pain (by Riley Finn)
5. Mr. Billowy Coat (by Riley Finn)

HISTORY OF ANGEL

HE'S BEEN AROUND FOR A LONG, LONG TIME

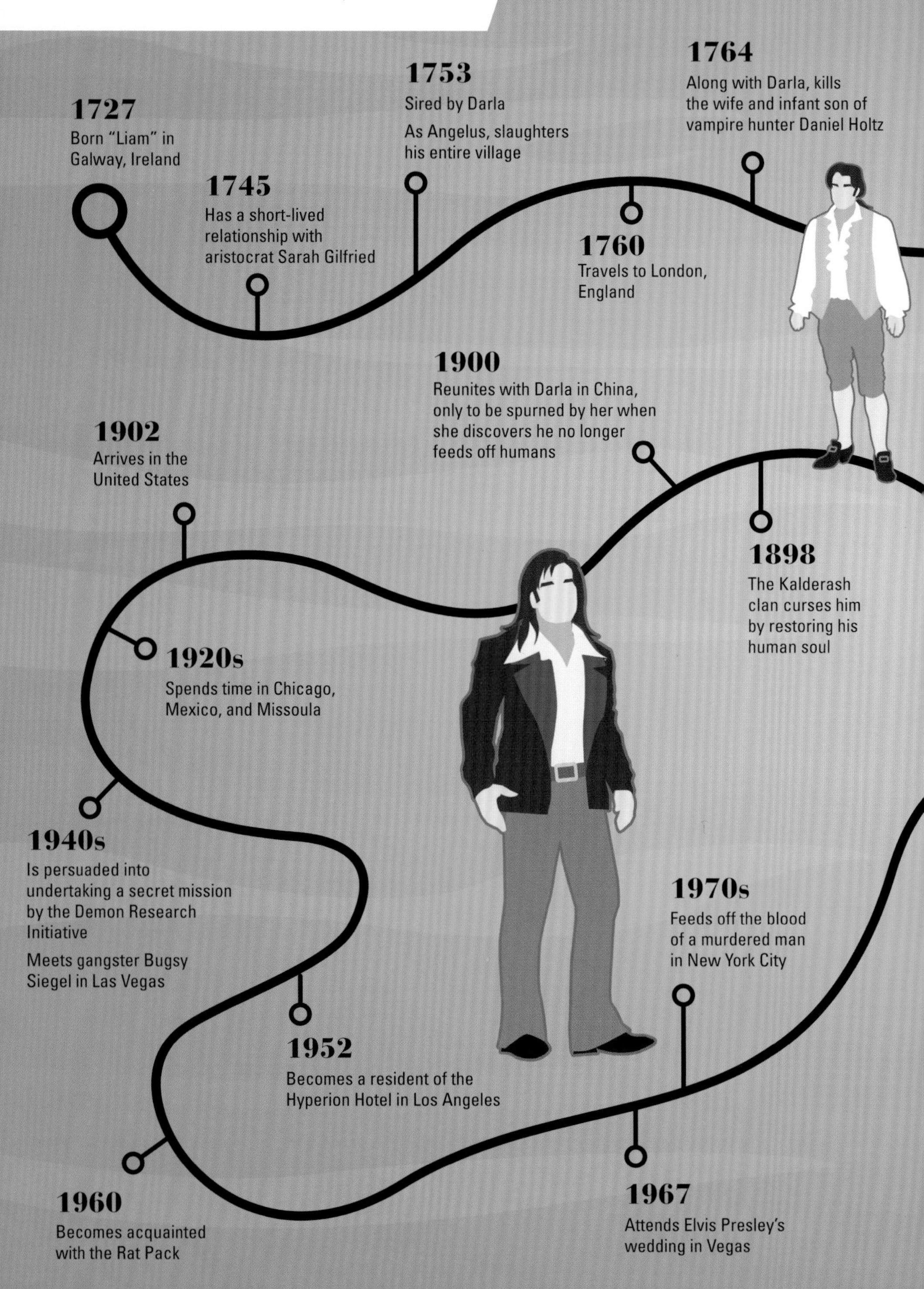

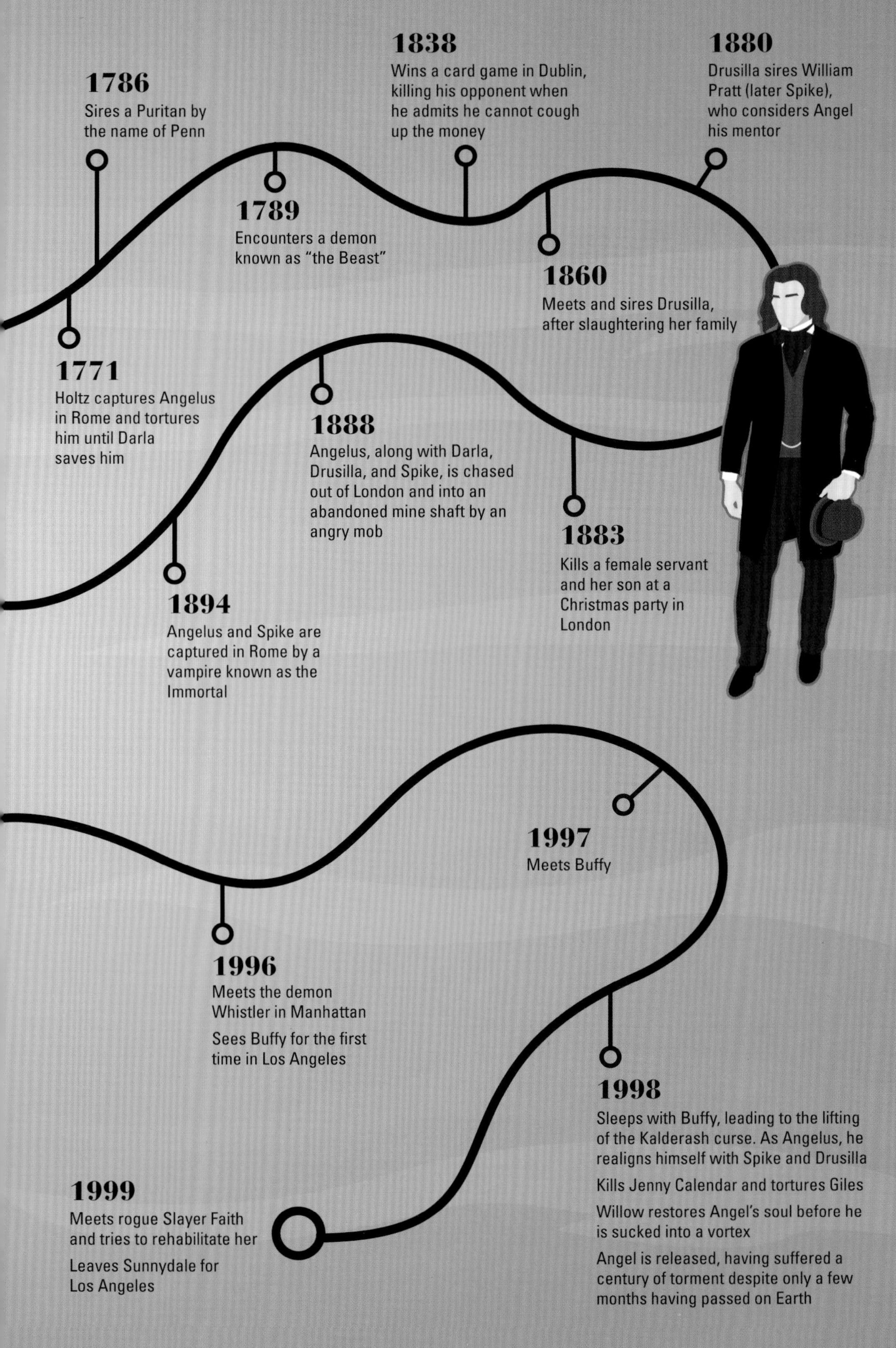

1771
Holtz captures Angelus in Rome and tortures him until Darla saves him
1786
Sires a Puritan by the name of Penn
1789
Encounters a demon known as "the Beast"
1838
Wins a card game in Dublin, killing his opponent when he admits he cannot cough up the money
1860
Meets and sires Drusilla, after slaughtering her family
1880
Drusilla sires William Pratt (later Spike), who considers Angel his mentor
1883
Kills a female servant and her son at a Christmas party in London
1888
Angelus, along with Darla, Drusilla, and Spike, is chased out of London and into an abandoned mine shaft by an angry mob
1894
Angelus and Spike are captured in Rome by a vampire known as the Immortal
1996
Meets the demon Whistler in Manhattan
Sees Buffy for the first time in Los Angeles
1997
Meets Buffy
1998
Sleeps with Buffy, leading to the lifting of the Kalderash curse. As Angelus, he realigns himself with Spike and Drusilla
Kills Jenny Calendar and tortures Giles
Willow restores Angel's soul before he is sucked into a vortex
Angel is released, having suffered a century of torment despite only a few months having passed on Earth
1999
Meets rogue Slayer Faith and tries to rehabilitate her
Leaves Sunnydale for Los Angeles

HOW TO DATE AN ANGEL

COULD YOU DO BETTER THAN BUFFY IN THE ROMANCE STAKES?

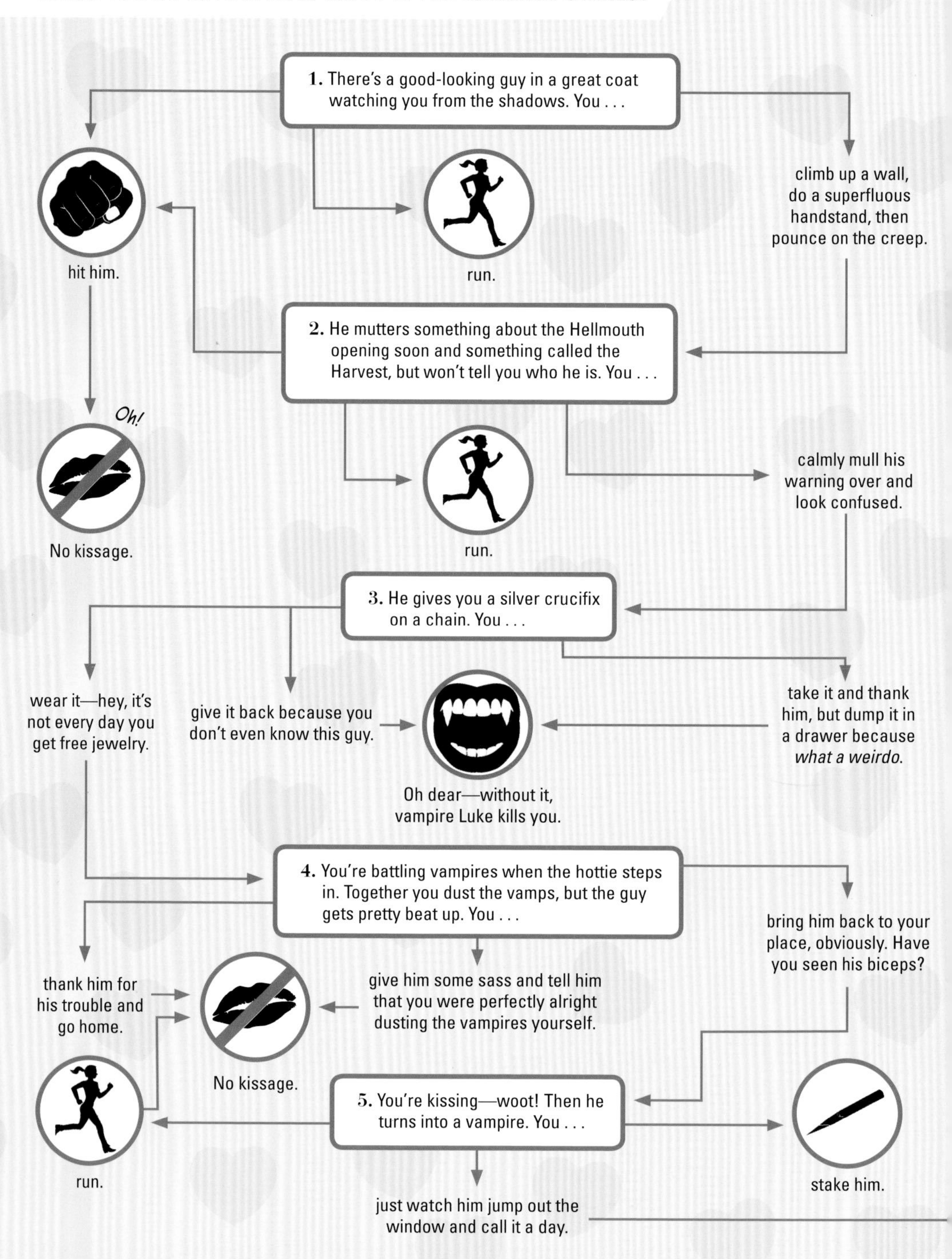

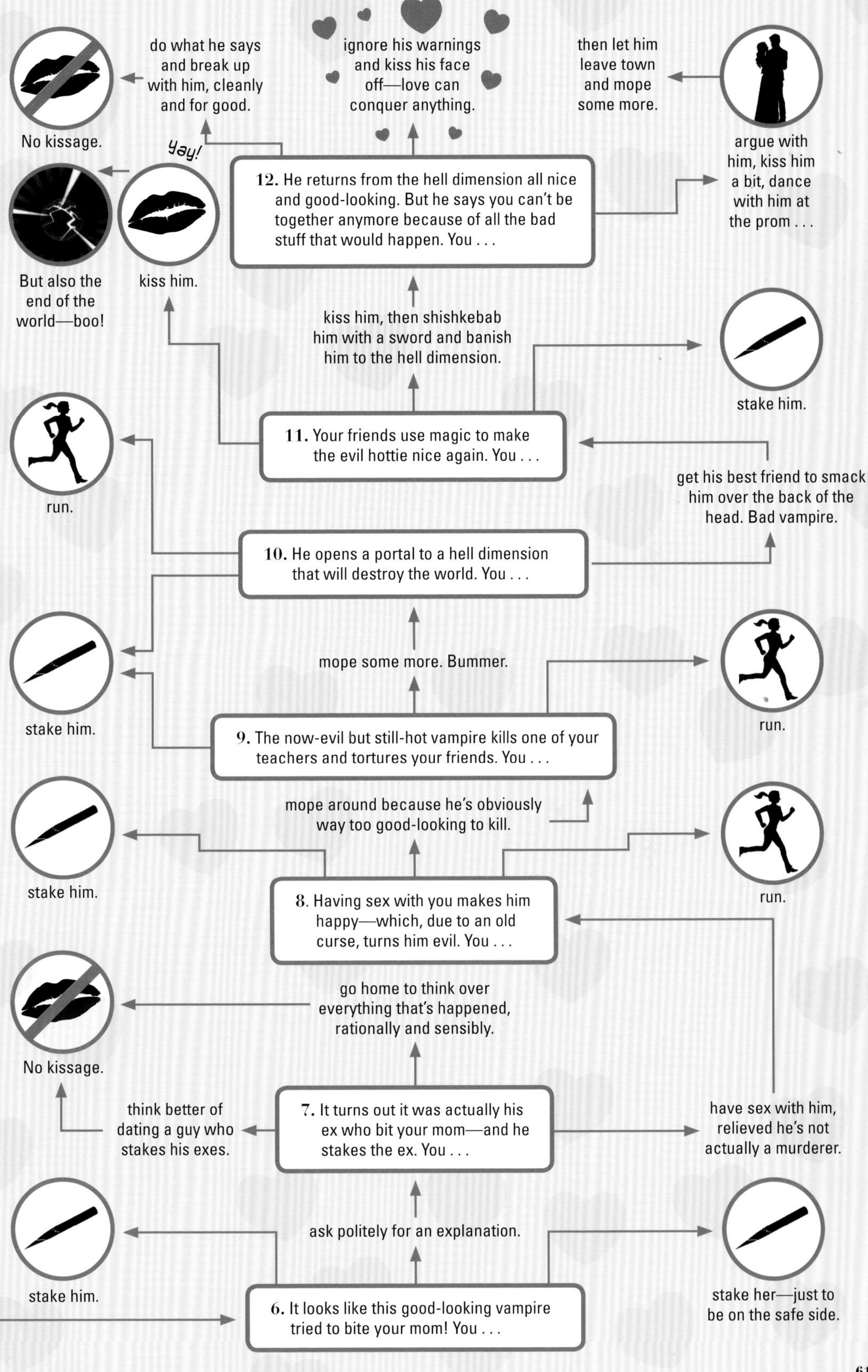

do what he says and break up with him, cleanly and for good.
ignore his warnings and kiss his face off—love can conquer anything.
then let him leave town and mope some more.
No kissage.
Yay!
12. He returns from the hell dimension all nice and good-looking. But he says you can't be together anymore because of all the bad stuff that would happen. You . . .
argue with him, kiss him a bit, dance with him at the prom . . .
But also the end of the world—boo!
kiss him.
kiss him, then shishkebab him with a sword and banish him to the hell dimension.
stake him.
11. Your friends use magic to make the evil hottie nice again. You . . .
run.
get his best friend to smack him over the back of the head. Bad vampire.
10. He opens a portal to a hell dimension that will destroy the world. You . . .
mope some more. Bummer.
stake him.
run.
9. The now-evil but still-hot vampire kills one of your teachers and tortures your friends. You . . .
mope around because he's obviously way too good-looking to kill.
stake him.
run.
8. Having sex with you makes him happy—which, due to an old curse, turns him evil. You . . .
go home to think over everything that's happened, rationally and sensibly.
No kissage.
think better of dating a guy who stakes his exes.
7. It turns out it was actually his ex who bit your mom—and he stakes the ex. You . . .
have sex with him, relieved he's not actually a murderer.
ask politely for an explanation.
stake him.
stake her—just to be on the safe side.
6. It looks like this good-looking vampire tried to bite your mom! You . . .

JOYCE AND DAWN SUMMERS

SUMMERS WOMEN ARE TOUGH

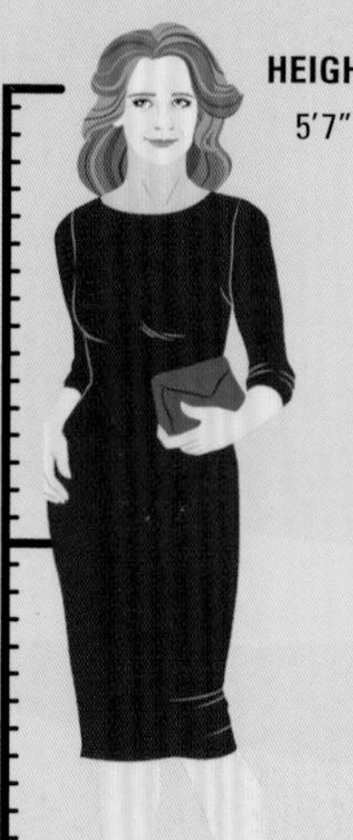

HEIGHT
5′7″

FIRST WORDS

"Now you have a good time. I know you'll make friends right away. Think positive. And honey . . . try not to get kicked out."
1-01 Welcome to the Hellmouth

LAST WORDS

"On the dessert cart!"
5-15 I Was Made to Love You

1997

Moves to Sunnydale, where she runs an art gallery

Dates Ted Buchanan, who she later discovers is a robot

1998

Becomes besotted with Xander (due to a spell)

Has a one-night stand with Giles (due to a spell)

DAWN EPISODE COUNT
66
(46%)

LOVES

Anchovies (her favorite pizza topping)

Her sister (sometimes)

Harry Potter

HATES

Being younger than everyone else

Her sister (sometimes)

Not being "real"

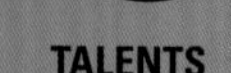

TALENTS

Casting spells (a bit)

Stealing

Killing vampires

2000

"Born"

CRUSHES

Justin

Xander

Spike

RJ

2001

Discovers her true identity as "the Key"

Becomes a kleptomaniac for a short time

Is kidnapped by Glory

Has first kiss with a vampire named Justin; later dusts him

LOVES
Buffy
Dawn
Her art gallery
Passions
Thelma & Louise
Seals and Crofts
Burt Reynolds

HATES
Jell-O

58
(40%)
JOYCE EPISODE COUNT

4
Number of episodes Joyce appears in *after* she died

LOVE INTERESTS
Hank Summers (married, divorced)
Ted
Xander (love spell)
Giles (candy spell)
Dracula (coffee date)

TALENTS
Running her art gallery
Being a mom
Caring for Buffy's friends

1999
Tries to burn Buffy (due to a spell—again)

2000
Diagnosed with a brain tumor

2001
Dies of a brain aneurysm

14
Age of Dawn when we first meet her

FIRST WORDS
"Mom!"
5-01 Buffy vs. Dracula

LAST WORDS
"Yeah, Buffy. What are we gonna do now?"
7-22 Chosen

HEIGHT
5′7½″

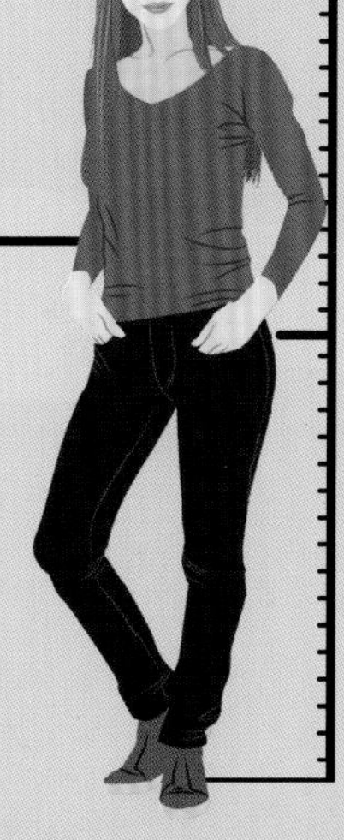

2002
Enrolls at Sunnydale High School
Becomes the victim of a love spell cast by a fellow student
Helps the Scooby gang defeat the First

ALIAS
The Key
"Human, now, and helpless."
The last Monk of Dagon to Buffy, in
5-05 No Place Like Home

FAMILY OR BLOOD TIES

BUFFY SPENDS FOUR SEASONS AS AN ONLY CHILD, BUT HOW MUCH BETTER IS A BIGGER FAMILY? WELL, IT'S RELATIVE . . .

XANDER

While Xander battles demons, his family members battle each other.

- Jessica Harris — Anthony Harris
 - Alexander Lavelle Harris
- Rory Harris (Uncle)
 - Carol Harris (Cousin) — Multiple husbands
 - Karen Harris
- Dave (Uncle)

BUFFY

They're so close-knit that loss hurts all the more.

- Arlene (Joyce's sister)
- Joyce Summers — Hank Summers — Hank's secretary
 - Buffy Anne Summers
 - Dawn Summers
- Celia (Cousin)

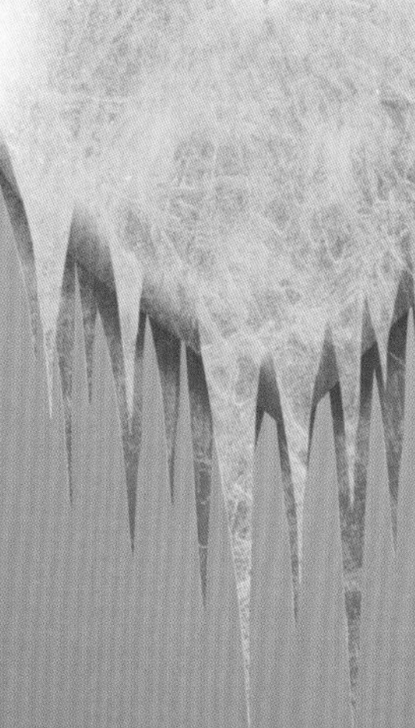

WILLOW

Brr, did it just get chilly in here?

- Sheila Rosenberg — Ira Rosenberg
 - Willow Danielle Rosenberg

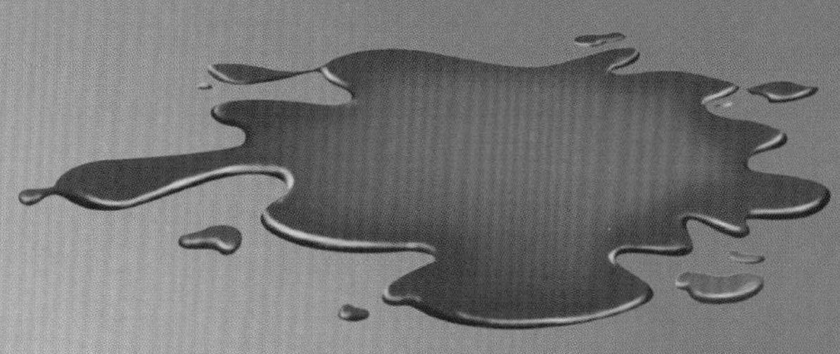

ANGEL

Not a happy family, even before Angel was a vampire.

Unknown killed by Angel — Unknown killed by Angel

Liam (aka Angel)

Kathy

GILES

Quintessential man of mystery.

??? — Rupert Edmund Giles — ???

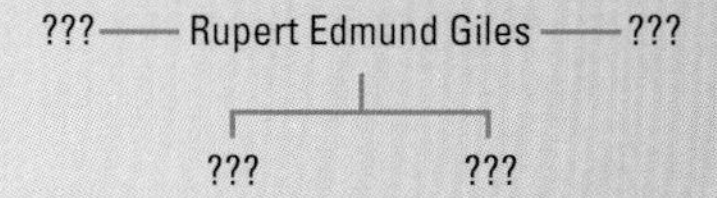

???

???

SPIKE

All we know is he's a mommy's boy.

Anne Pratt

William Pratt (aka Spike)

TARA

You have no right to interfere with Tara's blood kin.

Mrs. Maclay

Mr. Maclay

Tara Maclay

Donald Maclay

Beth Maclay (Cousin)

THE COST OF SLAYAGE

VAMPIRES CAN ONLY ENTER YOUR HOME IF INVITED, SO HOW DOES BUFFY'S HOUSE KEEP GETTING TRASHED?

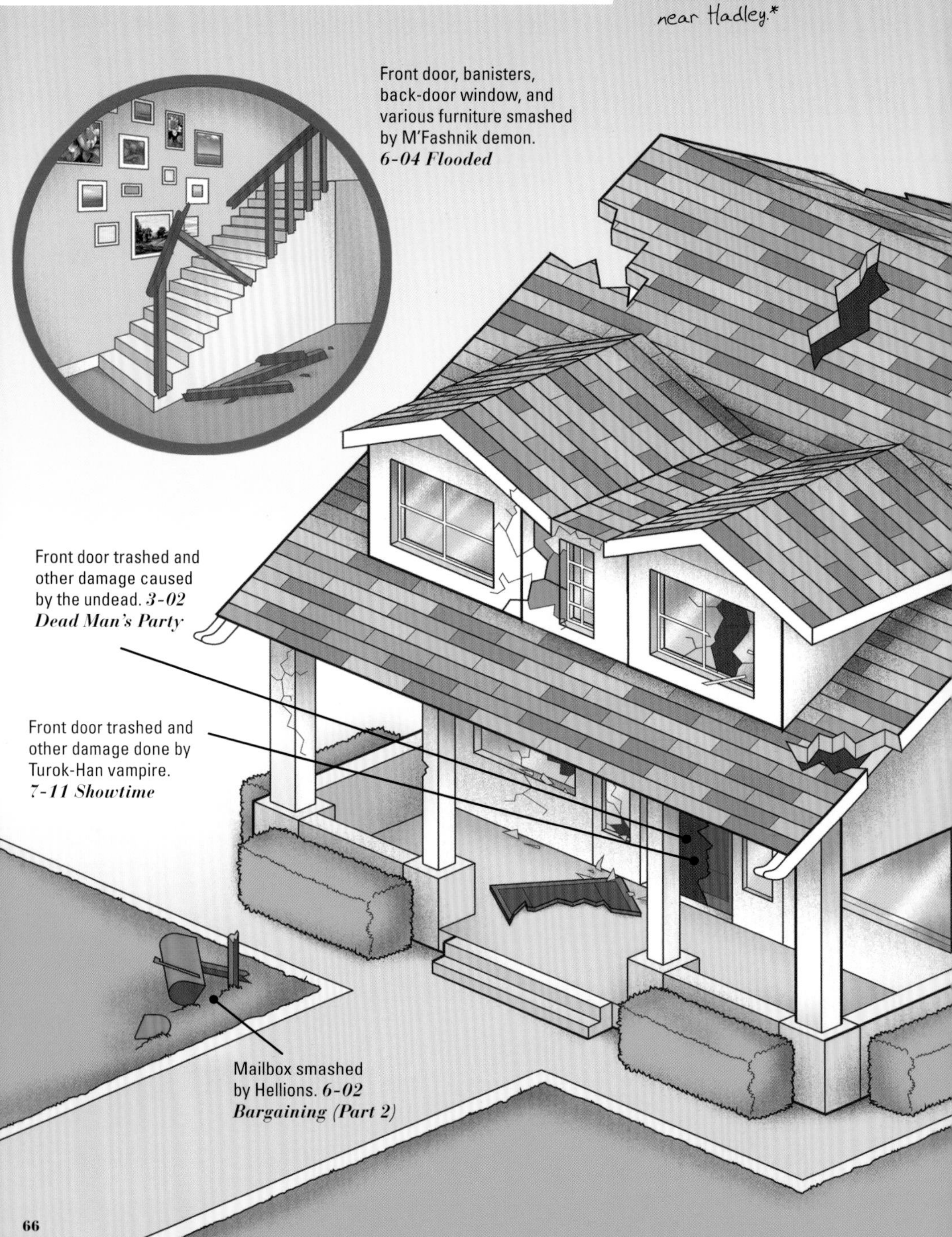

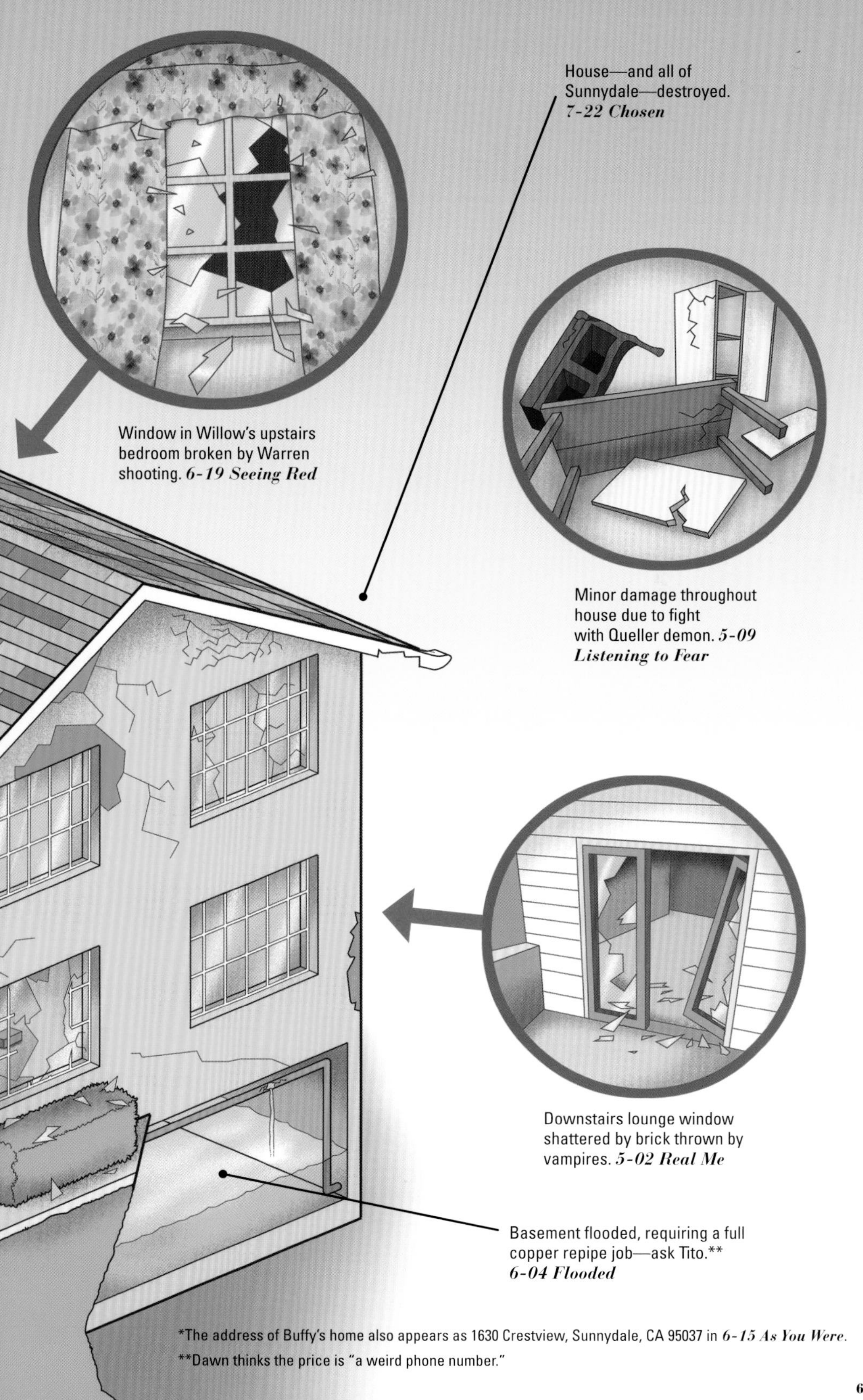

*The address of Buffy's home also appears as 1630 Crestview, Sunnydale, CA 95037 in *6-15 As You Were*.

**Dawn thinks the price is "a weird phone number."

SADDEST MOMENTS

Sad (adj.)

1. Feeling or showing sorrow
2. Pathetic, uncool, or awkward
3. Xander, according to Cordelia

Giles discovers Jenny Calendar's body

Buffy kills Angel

Willow breaks up with Oz

Cassie Newton drops dead at Buffy's feet

Willow tries to get her mom's attention by coming out as a witch

Joyce's death

WEEPY

Buffy's sacrifice to save Dawn

Tara's death

Buffy tells Spike she loves him just as he's about to die

Buffy disowns Giles

Anya's death

Spike's addiction to soap operas

Everything about Jonathan

Wesley's hesitation in asking Cordelia for a dance

Robot April's death

AWKWARD

Giles sings a very emotional song at the Espresso Pump

Xander meets his own über-successful double

Angel gets jealous of Spike's soul

BIG BATTLES— A SHARED DREAM

4-22 RESTLESS

1. Buffy, Willow, Xander, and Giles invoke the power of Sineya, the first Slayer, and use it to defeat Adam. (36:00 into ***4-21 Primeval***)

2. Willow dreams of her own insecurities and is attacked by Sineya. (12:06)

3. Xander dreams of his own insecurities and has his heart ripped out by Sineya. (25:14)

4. Giles dreams of his own insecurities and is knifed in the head by Sineya. (31:05)

5. Buffy dreams of her own insecurities and is attacked by Sineya. (39:02)

6. Buffy refuses to be intimidated and saves her friends. (40:05)

KEY DATES

[date unknown]
Sineya is the first Slayer.

THE HORROR, THE HORROR

Willow dreams of having to perform on stage in front of everyone she knows. Waaah!

Xander dreams of being seduced by Joyce. Weird!

Giles dreams of singing at the Bronze. It's quite nice, really.

THE HIGH COST OF WINNING

It's all a dream—isn't it?

SPIKE / WILLIAM

A QUICK LOOK AT THE SHOW'S ULTIMATE BAD BOY

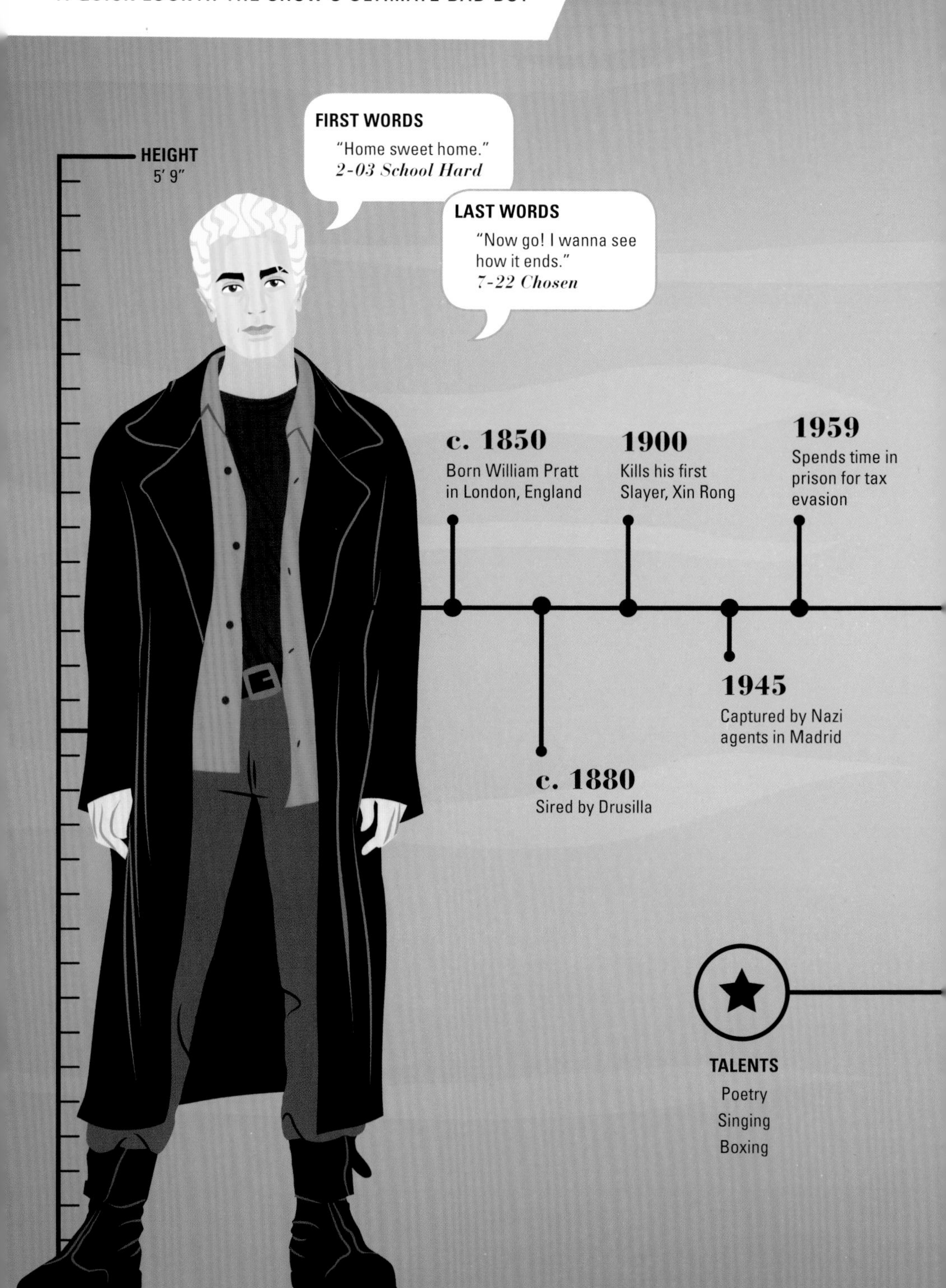

LOVES
Weetabix
Punk rock
Buffy

HATES
Angel
Pipe organs
Halloween

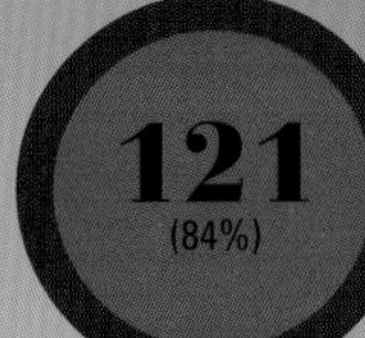

121 (84%)
EPISODE COUNT

1963
Kills two members of the Watchers' Council

1969
Attends Woodstock

1977
Kills his second Slayer, Nikki Woods

1997
Arrives in Sunnydale after being attacked in Prague

Is crushed by a collapsing pipe organ, leaving him paralyzed

1999
Hooks up with Sunnydale High student–turned-vampire Harmony Kendall

Is captured by the Initiative and has a cerebral microchip implanted in his skull

2000
Starts having erotic dreams about Buffy

2001
Begins an affair with Buffy

2002
Travels to Africa and has his soul returned

2003
Sacrifices himself to destroy the Turok-Han and close the Hellmouth

ROMANTIC QUESTS
Buffy
Drusilla
Buffybot
Cecily Addams

ALSO KNOWN AS
William the Bloody, after the "bloody awful" poetry he wrote in his lifetime

FOOLS FOR LOVE

THE BEST AND WORST PICK-UP LINES HEARD IN SUNNYDALE

I did a lot of thinking today. I really can't be around you. Because when I am . . . when I am, all I can ever think about is how badly I want to kiss you. (to Buffy) ***1-07 Angel***

You know, Buffy, uh, Spring Fling is a time for students to gather and . . . Oh, God! Buffy, I want you to go to the dance with me. You and me, on a date. (to Buffy) ***1-12 Prophecy Girl***

Sometimes when I'm sitting in class . . . you know, I'm not thinking about class, 'cause that would never happen. I think about kissing you. And it's like everything stops. It's like—it's like freeze frame. Willow kissage. (to Willow) ***2-14 Innocence***

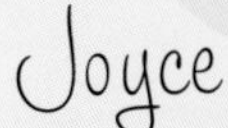

You are so cool. You're like Burt Reynolds. (to Giles) ***3-06 Band Candy***

I like you. You're funny and you're nicely shaped. And frankly it's ludicrous to have these interlocking bodies and not interlock. Please remove your clothing now. (to Xander) ***4-03 The Harsh Light of Day***

Parker

I've yet to find the girl that I can just sit with. Feel totally at ease. Feeling whatever's on my mind. Or even sit with comfortably in silence. Willow, can I tell you something kinda private? Just that I've enjoyed talking to you. Here. Tonight. (to Willow) ***4-05 Beer Bad***

Did Willow tell you I like cheese? (to Buffy) ***4-07 The Initiative***

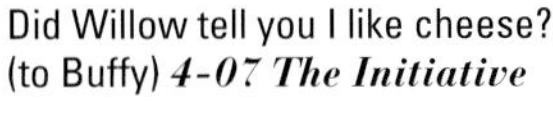

Riley

A funny thing happened with my prior social engagement. Pretty much ended when a friend of mine went off to do something with another crowd she hangs out with. Irony is kind of ironic that way. Anyway, I know it's late, but I thought maybe, I mean, if you still wanted to do something? (to Tara) ***4-13 The I in Team***

Willow

My heart expands,
'Tis grown a bulge in it,
Inspired by your beauty, effulgent.
(to Cecily) ***5-07 Fool for Love***

Spike

Okay, I dig the way you always turn off the *Moulin Rouge!* DVD at Chapter 32 so it has a happy ending. I like the way you speak; it's interesting. And your freckles . . . lickable. I'm not so into the magic stuff. It seems like fairy-tale crap to me, but if it matters to you . . . You care about it, so it's cool. (to Willow) ***7-13 The Killer in Me***

Kennedy

DEAD THINGS

"I MAY BE DEAD, BUT I'M STILL PRETTY."

—BUFFY, *1-12 PROPHECY GIRL*

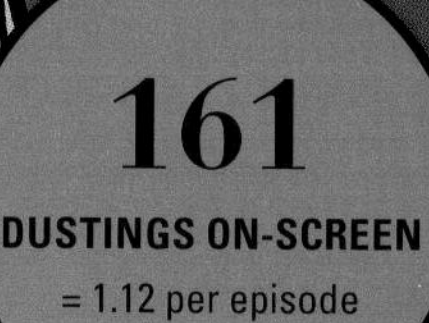

161

DUSTINGS ON-SCREEN

= 1.12 per episode

15

EPISODES IN WHICH NO ONE DIES

1-03 Witch
1-10 Nightmares
1-11 Out of Mind, Out of Sight
2-02 Some Assembly Required
4-02 Living Conditions
4-03 The Harsh Light of Day
4-07 The Initiative
4-12 A New Man
4-22 Restless
5-17 Forever
5-18 Intervention
6-09 Smashed
6-11 Gone
7-13 The Killer in Me
7-19 Empty Places

7

SIRINGS ON-SCREEN

1-02 The Harvest—Luke sires Jesse McNally
1-05 Never Kill a Boy On a First Date—Unnamed vampire sires Andrew Borba
2-07 Lie to Me—Spike sires Billy Fordham
2-15 Phases—Angel sires Theresa Klusmeyer
2-21 Becoming (Part 1)—Darla sires Angel
5-07 Fool for Love—Drusilla sires Spike
7-08 Sleeper—Spike sires an unnamed woman

574

DEATHS IN THE SERIES

Other deaths 240—41.81%

Buffy kills 212—36.93%

Spike kills 70—12.2%

Willow kills 14.5*—2.53%

Angel kills 14—2.44%

Giles kills 12—2.09%

Xander kills 11.5*—2%

*In *3-09 The Wish*, Xander and Willow kill Cordelia, scoring half a kill each.

Sunnyd

Vol. II No. 26

MIRACULOUS CURES FOR VAMPIRISM

ARE YOU:

* AFFLICTED BY FANGS?
* BLIGHTED BY BLOOD-LUST?
* SUDDENLY FEELING THE IMPULSE TO RUTHLESSLY EAT YOUR LOVED ONES?

Then, you, Sir or Madame, surely suffer from **VAMPIRISM**, an ancient and respectable malady but outwith the conventional Books and Education of leading medical men. Oh, woe and again woe—the Doctors cannot help you. What are you to do? Who are you to turn to? Permit us to offer these **TRUSTED** and **PROVEN** remedies for your unfortunate condition.

THE KALDERASH CURSE

Developed by Kalderash gypsies in Romania, this highly potent magic was used to full and evident effect in 1898 on the infamous vampire Angelus, restoring his soul.

The patented method uses an **Orb of Thesulah**—a spirit vault for the Rituals of the Undead.

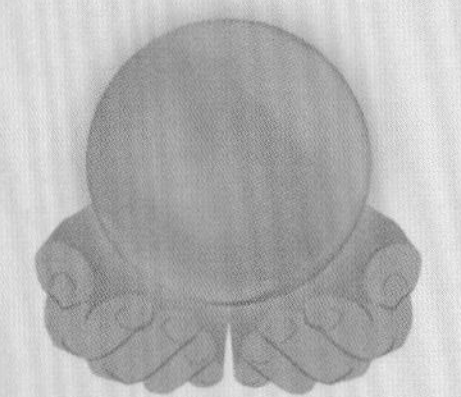

Nici mort nici al fiintei te invoc, spirit al trécerii. Reda trupului ce separa omul de animal. Asa sa fie.	*Not dead, nor of the living. Spirits of the interregnum, I call. Restore to the corporal vessel that which separates us from beast. So shall it be.*

Warning: A moment of pure happiness such as "full intimacy" with another Person may render a premature end to this curse. We can take no responsibility for any resultant maiming, torture, or embarrassment.

AFRICAN TRIALS

This Adventurous Excursion is not for the faint-hearted, but promises a full cure. Simply complete a series of tasks for a discretely unnamed demon in a cave in Uganda and your soul will be returned. The trials include:

- Fight to death with a man whose hands are on fire
- Fight to death with at least two other demons
- Endure a plague of insects and beetles in your nose and mouth

Do please note that these trials—and the trip to sunny Africa—have a high risk of death or permanent injury. The return of your soul may lead to madness, and we cannot vouchsafe that it will mean any person will now reciprocate any amatory feelings.

LETHE'S BRAMBLE

A remarkable remedy with none of the Inherent Dangers of other so-called cures! Simply FORGET that you're a vampire!!!

e Press

Thursday, January 19, 1899

QUICK! SIMPLE! EFFECTIVE!

Lethe's Bramble is a Natural and Organic herb.

The preparation: Dry the sprigs, burn them, and then touch them with the white crystal WE will supply, while reciting this easily remembered incantation:

Let Lethe's Bramble do its chore. Purge their minds of memories grim, of pains from recent slights and sins . . .

When the fire goes out. When the crystal turns black. The spell will be cast.

Tabula rasa. Tabula rasa. Tabula rasa.

The crystal will turn GRAY on contact with the herbs, and BLACK when the enchantment has worked.

BOTTLE IT

Cheap, effective alternative to biting people. Available from all over-worked hospitals where security is a bit lax.

STAKE

Cure your vampirism the traditional way! Heartily endorsed by the Watchers' Council of Britain.

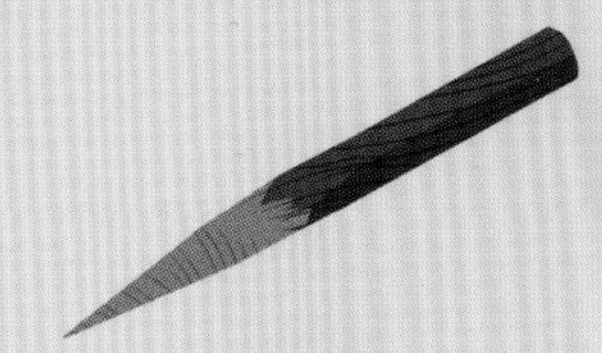

HOLIDAY

If you're not minded to CURE your condition, perhaps you just want a change of scene. Sorcerer **Richard Wilkins** has newly established the town of Sunnydale in California with convenient views of the Hellmouth.

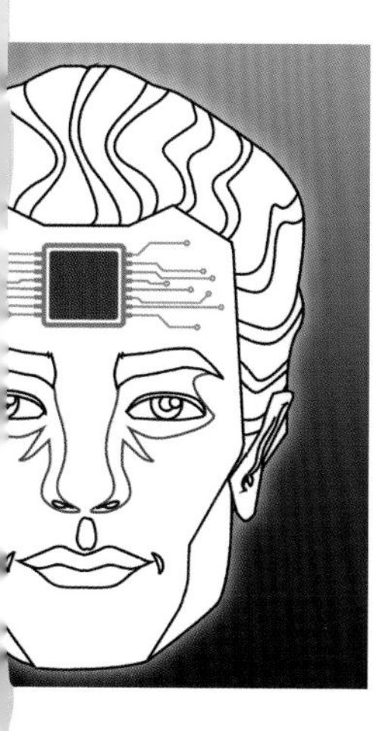

STOP VAMPIRES WITH CHIPS

FAO all agents: Professor Walsh reports positive results from the first deployed use of the BEHAVIOR-MODIFICATION CIRCUITRY on a Hostile Subterranean. When the "chip" was surgically implanted onto the brain of Hostile 17, any attempt at violence directed at a human caused Hostile 17 severe neurological pain.

The chip does not affect HSTs in conflict with other HSTs, which may mean treated subjects can be conditioned for work on dangerous operations. Professor Walsh estimates that, from implantation, each chip will operate for two years before terminating the subject. "Frankly, there's no downside," says Walsh. "It's another proof of concept as we work towards realization of the 314 Project."

TOP SECRET
INITIATIVES EYES ONLY

BIG BATTLES—GLORY

5-22 THE GIFT

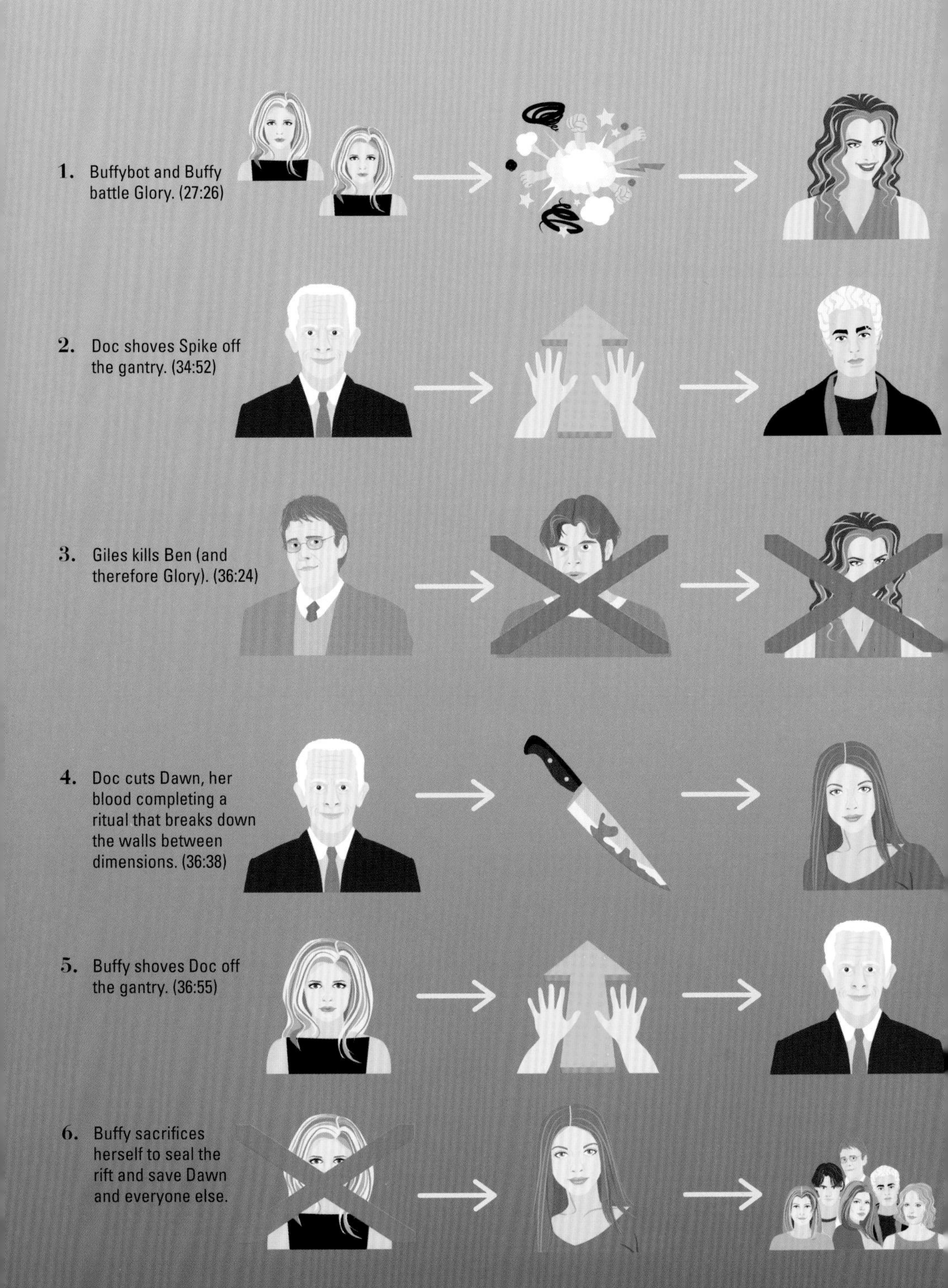

KEY DATES

[date unknown]

Glorificus rules a hell dimension with two other hellgods, who become afraid of her growing power and cruelty. A battle erupts between them.

c. 1976

The hellgods banish Glorificus to Earth, where she is forced to live and die in the body of newborn Ben Wilkinson.

2000

Monks of the Order of Dragon find the Key of living energy that can shatter the walls between dimensions, allowing Glory to get home. To hide the Key, the monks turn it into a sister for Buffy—Dawn.

2001

Glory finds Dawn.

THE HORROR, THE HORROR

Dawn is cut and bled to open the rift

Spike is thrown from the gantry

THE HIGH COST OF WINNING

Giles kills the innocent Ben

Bricks fall on Anya

Buffy dies

Sooner or later Glory will reemerge and make Buffy pay for that mercy. And the world with her. Buffy even knows that and still she couldn't take a human life. She's a hero, you see. She's not like us.

Once the key is activated, it won't just open the gates to the beast's dimension. It's going to open all the gates. The walls separating realities will crumble. Dimensions will bleed into each other. Order will be overthrown and the universe will tumble into chaos. All dark, forever.

DANIEL "OZ" OSBOURNE AND CORDELIA CHASE

THE COOLEST WEREWOLF AND THE ULTIMATE QUEEN BEE

HEIGHT
5'4"

FIRST WORDS
"Of what?"
2-04 Inca Mummy Girl

LAST WORDS
"Pretty much now."
4-19 New Moon Rising

DINGOES ATE MY BABY

A favorite act at the Bronze

Singer: Devon MacLeish

Guitar: Daniel "Oz" Osbourne

"There's a quiet restraint and total lack of bitterness to [Oz's] sarcasm; where Devon is your typical excitable rock and roller, Oz is completely unflappable. His is the kind of cool that is completely unaware of itself."

Description of Oz in the script for *2-04 Inca Mummy Girl*

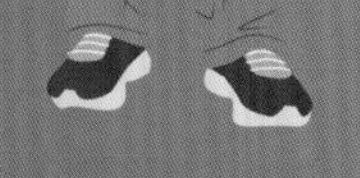

CORDELIA EPISODE COUNT

56
(39%)

LOVES
Whitney Houston
Attention
Money

HATES
Nerds
Libraries
Tact

THE CORDETTES
Cordelia's popular clique

Harmony Kendall
Gwen Ditchik
Aura
Aphrodesia

LOVE CHART

Jesse McNally
Guy Matthews
John Lee Walker
Richard Anderson
Owen Thurman
Mitch Fargo
Wesley Wyndam-Pryce
Angel
Kevin Benedict
Xander Harris

1997

Meets and initially befriends Buffy

Runs for May Queen

Kidnapped by Sunnydale student Chris Epps

Nearly sacrificed to the demon Machida

Kisses Xander for the first time

LOVES

Sleep
(when he can get it)

Willow

Music

HATES

Talking

Tara

Full moons

40
(28%)

OZ EPISODE COUNT

4
Nights per month that Oz spends as a werewolf

TALENTS

Playing guitar

Powerful sense of smell

Quiet sarcasm

1997

First sees Willow (dressed as an Eskimo at the Bronze)

Starts dating Willow

1998

Discovers he has become a werewolf after being bitten by his cousin

Breaks up with Willow after seeing her kiss Xander

Gets back together with Willow

1999

Enrolls at UC Sunnydale as a psychology student

Willow discovers he has cheated on her with Veruca, a fellow werewolf

Kills Veruca after she threatens to kill Willow

Leaves Sunnydale

2000

Returns to Sunnydale from Tibet and is captured by the Initiative

After being rescued by Buffy and Riley, leaves Sunnydale again

TALENTS

Cheerleading

Color coordination

Makeup

FIRST WORDS

"Here."
1-01 Welcome to the Hellmouth

LAST WORDS

"I'm for it."
3-21 Graduation Day (Part 1)

HEIGHT
5'7"

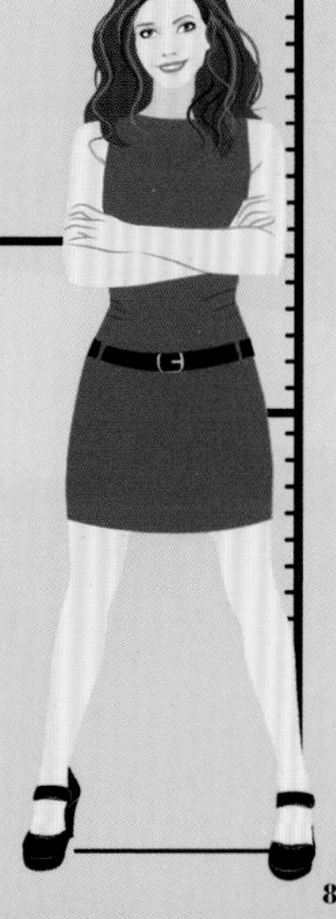

1998

Temporarily ends her affair with Xander on Valentine's Day

After witnessing Xander and Willow kiss, falls and impales herself

Breaks up with Xander once and for all

Wishes that Buffy had never come to Sunnydale and gets her wish granted by the demon Anyanka

1999

Begins working at the April Fools boutique

Is (badly) kissed twice by Wesley Wyndam-Pryce

Stakes her first vampire

Moves to Los Angeles after graduation to pursue an acting career

UNEXPECTED WISDOM

MANY IN THE SHOW ARE KNOWN FOR THEIR QUIPPY ELOQUENCE, BUT OZ AND CORDELIA REALLY DO DELIVER SOME OF THE PITHIEST, WITTIEST, SASSIEST LINES

Mom started borrowing my clothes. There should be an age limit on Lycra pants. *3-06 Band Candy*
Look, Buffy, you may be hot stuff when it comes to demonology or whatever, but when it comes to dating, I'm the Slayer. *2-06 Halloween*
I aspire to help my fellow man. Check. As long as he's not smelly, dirty, or something gross. *2-09 What's My Line (Part 1)*
Do you know what you need, Xander, besides a year's supply of acne cream? A brain. *2-08 The Dark Age*
Planning life as a loser? Most people just turn out that way, but you're really taking charge. *3-14 Bad Girls*

BANDS AT THE BRONZE

THE BRONZE IS THE ONLY CLUB IN SUNNYDALE WORTH GOING TO; EVEN IF THEY LET ANYBODY IN THERE, IT'S STILL THE SCENE. BUT WHO'S PLAYING?

THE BRO

NERF HERDER
DASHBOARD PROPHETS
SHY
DINGOES ATE MY BABY
AIMEE MANN
DARLING VIOLETTA
SPLENDID
CIBO MATTO
MICHELLE BRANCH
THE BREEDERS

"Man, I hate playing vampire towns!"
—Aimee Mann at the Bronze, *7-08 Sleeper*

E

NZE

ABERDEEN
BELLYLOVE
VELVET CHAIN
DEVICS
HALO FRIENDLIES
ANGIE HART

LOTION
NICKEL
SPRUNG MONKEY
VIRGIL
SUPERFINE

BUFFY: THE ALBUM JUKEBOX

BUFFY THE VAMPIRE SLAYER: THE ALBUM **WAS RELEASED BY TVT RECORDS ON OCTOBER 19, 1999**

No.	Song	Artist
1	**Buffy the Vampire Slayer Theme**	Nerf Herder
2	**Teenage FBI**	Guided by Voices
3	**Temptation Waits**	Garbage
4	**Strong**	Velvet Chain
5	**I Quit**	Hepburn
6	**Over My Head**	Furslid
7	**Lucky**	Bif Naked
8	**Keep Myself Awake**	Black Lab
9	**Virgin State of Mind**	K's Choice
10	**Already Met You**	Superfine
11	**The Devil You Know (God is a Man)**	Face to Face
12	**Nothing But You**	Kim Ferron
13	**It Doesn't Matter**	Alison Krauss & Union Station
14	**Wild Horses**	The Sundays
15	**Pain (Slayer Mix)**	Four Star Mary
16	**Charge**	Splendid
17	**Transylvanian Concubine**	Rasputina
18	**Close Your Eyes (Buffy/Angel Love Theme)**	Christophe Beck

A B C D E F G H J K

1 2 3 4 5 6 7 8 9 10

INSERT COIN PRESS THE RED BUTTON

1. **Buffy the Vampire Slayer Theme**
Nerf Herder

Featured in the opening credits of the show

Nerf Herder was formed in 1994. The band's name comes from a line from *The Empire Strikes Back*.

2. **Teenage FBI**
Guided by Voices

Not featured in the show

This song is included in the album *Do the Collapse*, released on August 3, 1999. Guided by Voices was formed in 1983, and its only founding member still in the band is singer-songwriter Robert Pollard.

3. **Temptation Waits**
Garbage

Not featured in the show

The song is from the album *Version 2.0*, released May 4, 1998. Garbage is also known for its James Bond theme *The World Is Not Enough*.

4. **Strong**
Velvet Chain

Featured in *1-05 Never Kill a Boy on the First Date*

This song is from the album *Warm*, released in December 1997.

5. **I Quit**
Hepburn

Not featured in the show

I Quit appears in the album *Hepburn*, released on August 30, 1999.

6. **Over My Head**
Furslide

Not featured in the show

The song is from the album *Adventure*, released on October 6, 1998. It was the band's only LP.

7. **Lucky**
Bif Naked

Featured in *4-03 The Harsh Light of Day*

The song is from the album *I Bificus*, released on February 24, 1998. Bif Naked is the nom-de-plume of Canadian singer-songwriter Beth Torbert.

8. **Keep Myself Awake**
Black Lab

Featured in *4-13 The I in Team*

Black Lab was formed in 1995 and is still active.

9. **Virgin State of Mind**
K's Choice

Featured in *4-16 Doppelgangland*

K's Choice is a Belgian rock band from Antwerp.

10. **Already Met You**
Superfine

Featured in *1-04 Teacher's Pet*

Already Met You appears in the EP *Superfine*.

11. **The Devil You Know (God Is a Man)**
Face to Face

Featured in *4-18 Where the Wild Things Are*

The song is from the album *Ignorance Is Bliss*, released on July 27, 1999.

12. **Nothing But You**
Kim Ferron

Featured in *4-05 Beer Bad*

The song was first released on *Buffy the Vampire Slayer: The Album*.

13. **It Doesn't Matter**
Alison Krauss & Union Station

Featured in *2-01 When She Was Bad*

The song appears in the album *So Long So Wrong*, released on March 25, 1997, winner of the Grammy Award for Best Bluegrass Album.

14. **Wild Horses**
The Sundays

Featured in *3-20 The Prom*

This cover of The Rolling Stones song was the B-side to The Sundays' 1992 single *Goodbye*.

15. **Pain (Slayer Mix)**
Four Star Mary

Featured in *2-16 Bewitched, Bothered and Bewildered*

Pain was released as a single in 2001. Three members of Four Star Mary are members of fictitious Buffy band Dingoes Ate My Baby.

16. **Charge**
Splendid

Featured in *2-19 I Only Have Eyes for You*

Splendid consisted of a married couple, Angie Hart and Jesse Tobias.

17. **Transylvanian Concubine**
Rasputina

Featured in *2-13 Surprise*

This song is from the EP *Transylvanian Regurgitations*, released on August 12, 1997.

18. **Close Your Eyes**
(Buffy/Angel Love Theme)
Christophe Beck

Featured in several episodes

The Canadian-born composer Christophe Beck won an Emmy in 1998 for his work on *Buffy the Vampire Slayer*.

Other albums based on the show:

Buffy the Vampire Slayer: Once More, with Feeling
(released by Rounder Records on September 24, 2002)

Buffy the Vampire Slayer: Radio Sunnydale—Music from the TV Series
(released by Virgin Records on September 30, 2003)

Buffy the Vampire Slayer: The Score
(released by Rounder Records on September 9, 2008)

TARA MACLAY

AT ONCE POWERFUL AND VULNERABLE, HER CHARMS ARE LIKE NO OTHER

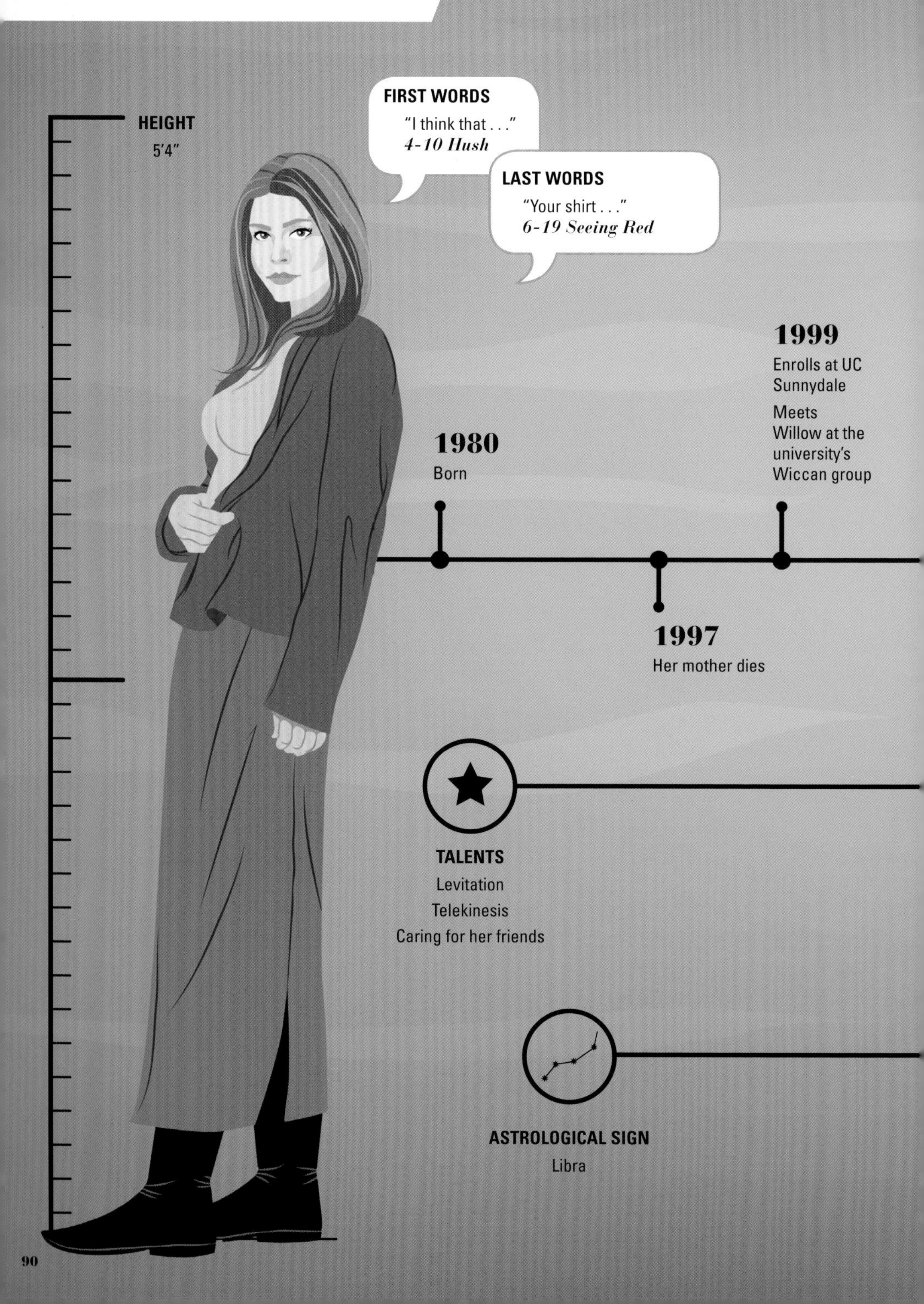

LOVES

Willow

Long skirts

Miss Kitty Fantastico

HATES

Shrimp (she's allergic)

People messing with her memory

Being the center of attention

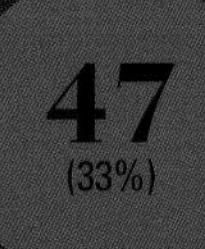

47
(33%)

EPISODE COUNT

2000

Tara's family arrives to tell her she must become a demon (like her mother), but she stands up to them

2001

Becomes mentally unstable when Glory feeds on her mind

Ends her relationship with Willow

2002

Gets back together with Willow

Is shot and killed by Warren Mears

Tara Maclay was voted number

15

in AfterEllen.com's "Top 50 Lesbian and Bisexual Characters" poll in 2010.

AMY VS. WILLOW VS. TARA

WHICH WITCH IS WHICH?

	AMY MADISON	WILLOW ROSENBERG	TARA MACLAY
	* When Willow first meets Amy, Amy is the far more powerful witch!		* When Willow first meets Tara, Tara is the far more powerful witch!
Descended from line of witches	✓		✓
Sunnydale High	✓	✓	
UC Sunnydale		✓	✓
Does dark magic	✓	✓	
Kills someone		✓	✓
Kills someone with magic		✓	
Most effective spell	Escapes being burned at the stake by turning herself into a rat. (3-11 Gingerbread)	She returns Angel's soul, brings Buffy back from the dead, and almost destroys the whole world. But Willow's greatest magic is when she uses the essence of the M? scythe to make every potential Slayer in the world into a fully fledged Slayer. (7-22 Chosen)	The first time she meets Buffy, she spots that the flow of her energy is fragmented—because Faith has swapped bodies with her. Willow and Tara then conjure a Draconian Katra to swap Buffy and Faith back. (4-16 Who Are You?)
Say what?	"Goddess Hecate, work thy will! Before thee let the unclean thing crawl!" (Amy turns herself into a rat, 3-11 Gingerbread)	"Te implor Doamne, nu ignora accasta rugamainte! Lasa orbita sa fie vasul care-l va transporta sufletul la el! Este scris, aceasta putere este dreptul poporuil meu de a conduce. . . Asa sa fie! Acum!" (Willow returns Angel's soul to him, 2-22 Becoming, Part 2)	"Blind Cadria, desolate queen, work my will upon them all, your curse upon them, my obeisance to you." (Tara makes demons invisible to her friends, 5-06 Family)
Least effective spell	A love spell intended to make Cordelia fall for Xander makes all women except Cordelia fall for Xander. (2-16 Bewitched, Bothered and Bewildered)	Magically controls a car she and Dawn are in as they are chased by a demon—only to smash the car into a pillar, fracturing Dawn's arm and almost killing them both. (6-10 Wrecked)	So Willow and the others don't find out that Tara is a demon, she casts a spell that makes demons invisible to them—which is no help when demons then attack. Anyway, Tara isn't a demon. (5-06 Family)

The spell works so well she remains a rat for three years (bar one brief reprieve).

FINAL VERDICT

AMY AND TARA ARE BOTH GIFTED WITCHES, BUT WILLOW . . . SHE'S A GODDESS (AS KENNEDY SAYS IN 7-22 CHOSEN).

ROOKIES?

THE OTHER SCOOBIES AND THEIR SKILLS AT MAGIC

Giles calls on Corsheth and Gilail to reverse the spell cast by Amy's mom Catherine; he says it's his first casting. (1-03 Witch)

Spike uses Angel's blood in a ritual of black medicine to heal Drusilla. (2-10 What's My Line, Part 2)

Angel easily transforms a fire into the Flame of Life. (3-07 Revelations)

Anya (with Willow's help) calls on Eryishon to retrieve her magic amulet from another dimension, but retrieves a vampire Willow instead. (3-16 Doppelgangland)

Oz inadvertently summons the demon Gachnar by bleeding on a magic symbol. (4-04 Fear, Itself)

Jonathan's augmentation spell makes people think he's one of the gang and a hero. (4-17 Superstar)

Buffy performs Cloutier's "Tirer la Couverture," a spell to see spells, and so learns that Dawn is not her sister. (5-05 No Place Like Home)

Dawn casts a resurrection spell that briefly brings her mother back to life. (5-17 Forever)

Xander summons an unnamed demon who makes everyone in Sunnydale sing and dance. (6-07 Once More, with Feeling)

THERE AND BACK AGAIN

DEATHS AND REBIRTHS IN SUNNYDALE

Buffy

1-12 Prophecy Girl

As prophesized in the Pergamum Codex, the Master kills Buffy and her blood frees him from imprisonment. Angel confirms that Buffy is dead.

Xander resuscitates Buffy using CPR, but she really was dead. As a result, a new Slayer—Kendra Young—is chosen.

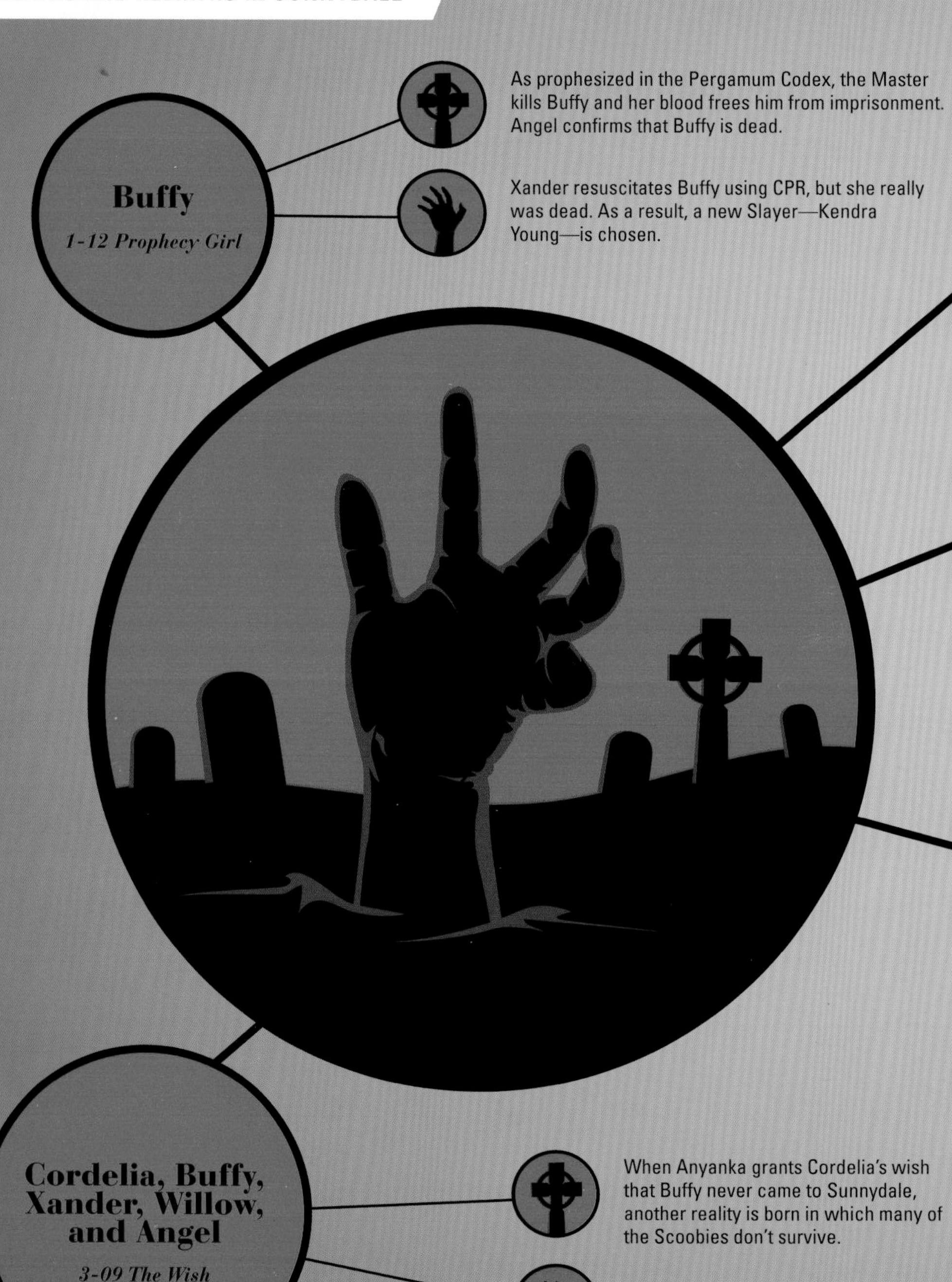

Cordelia, Buffy, Xander, Willow, and Angel

3-09 The Wish

When Anyanka grants Cordelia's wish that Buffy never came to Sunnydale, another reality is born in which many of the Scoobies don't survive.

Giles breaks Anyanka's amulet, returning things to normal.

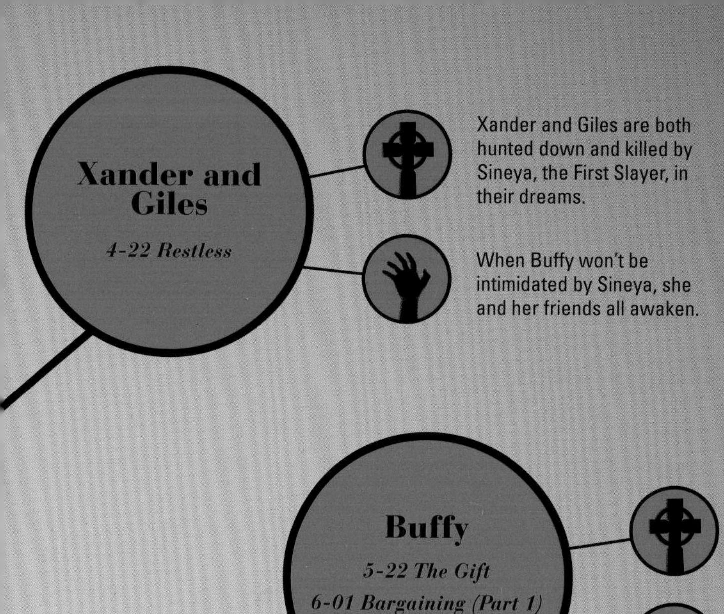

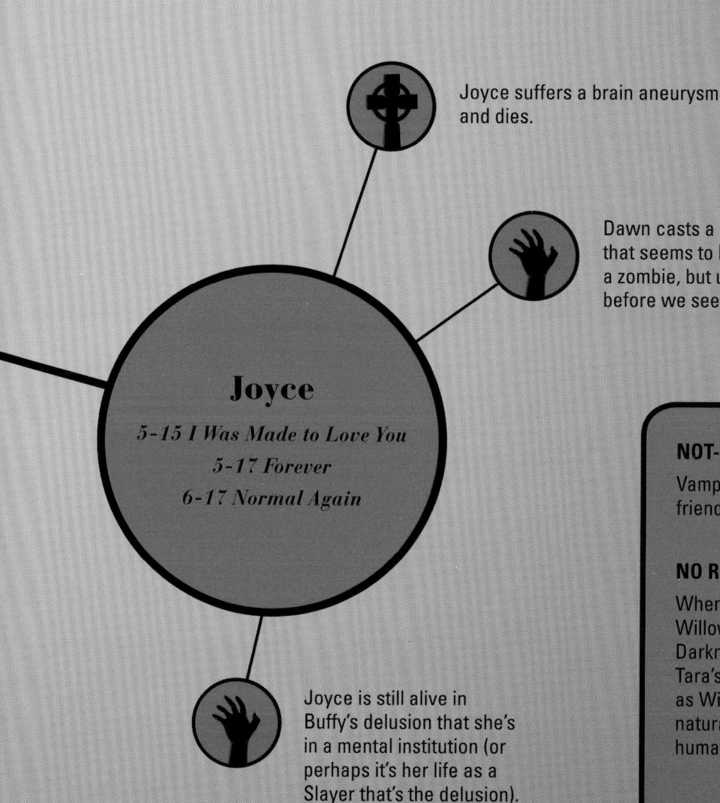

NOT-REALLY-HAPPY RETURNS

Vampire Jack O'Toole resurrects his dead friends as zombies in *3-13 The Zeppo.*

NO RETURNS

When her beloved Tara is murdered, Willow invokes Osiris, Keeper of Darkness, and demands the return of Tara's life. But even a witch as powerful as Willow cannot violate the laws of natural passing—a human death by human means. *(6-20 Villains)*

UC SUNNYDALE

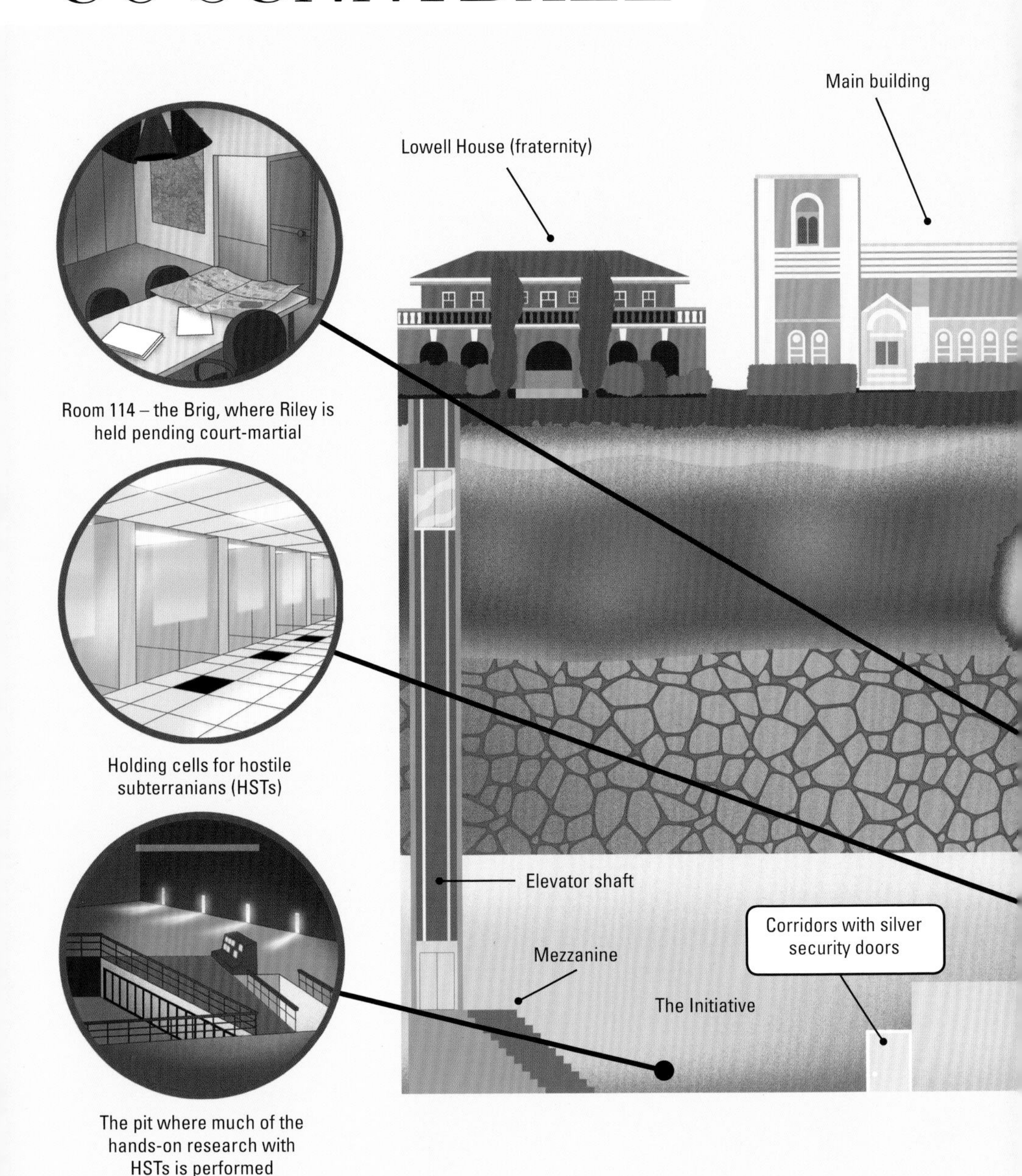

Room 114 – the Brig, where Riley is held pending court-martial

Holding cells for hostile subterranians (HSTs)

The pit where much of the hands-on research with HSTs is performed

1868
The University of California is founded and based in Oakland.

1873
The UC Berkeley campus is established.

c. 1961
UC Sunnydale is established.

Lowell Home for Children is taken over by the university for use as a fraternity house.

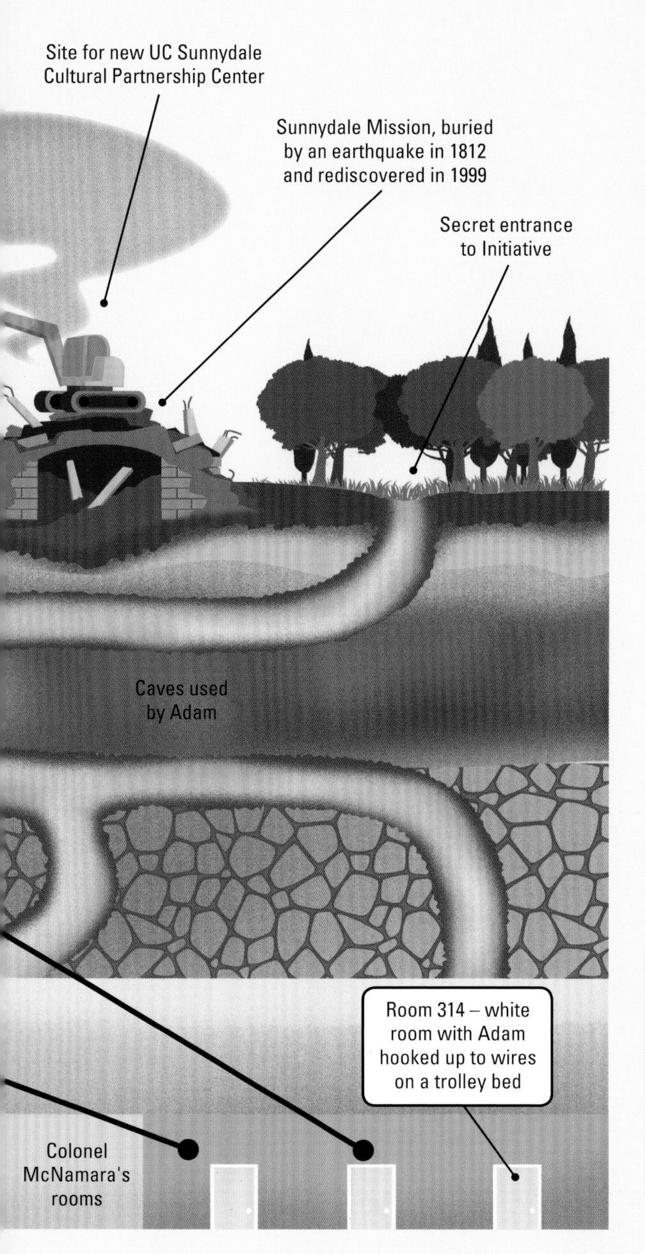

STAFF

(in alphabetical order)

Surrinda Blackmaster
Assistant to Dean Guerrero
Not seen, but rejects Buffy's application to be readmitted in ***6-15 As You Were***

Riley Finn
Teaching Assistant to Professor Walsh (see below)
First seen in ***4-01 The Freshman***

Professor Gerhardt
Anthropology teacher
Murdered by ghost of the Hus, ***4-08 Pangs***

Matthew Guerrero
Dean of UC Sunnydale
Seen in ***4-08 Pangs***

Professor Hawkins*
Seen in ***7-05 Selfless***

Professor Lillian
Poetry teacher
Seen in ***5-19 Tough Love***

Mike
Sociology teacher
Seen in ***6-05 Life Serial***

Professor Riegert
Popular American culture teacher
Seen in ***4-01 The Freshman***

Professor Roberts*
History teacher
Seen in ***5-12 Checkpoint***

Professor Maggie Walsh
Psychology teacher
First seen in ***4-01 The Freshman***
Murdered by Adam (her own creation) in ***4-13 The I in Team***

*Named in the shooting script, but not on-screen.

1999–2001
Buffy Summers attends UC Sunnydale.

2000
The government-sponsored Initiative, operating underneath the campus, is closed down.

2002
A Grimslaw demon rips the hearts from all the members of an unnamed fraternity at the behest of vengeance demon Anyanka, working on behalf of a student named Rachel.

2003
The UC Sunnydale campus is destroyed along with the rest of Sunnydale.

BIG BATTLES— DARK WILLOW

6-22 GRAVE

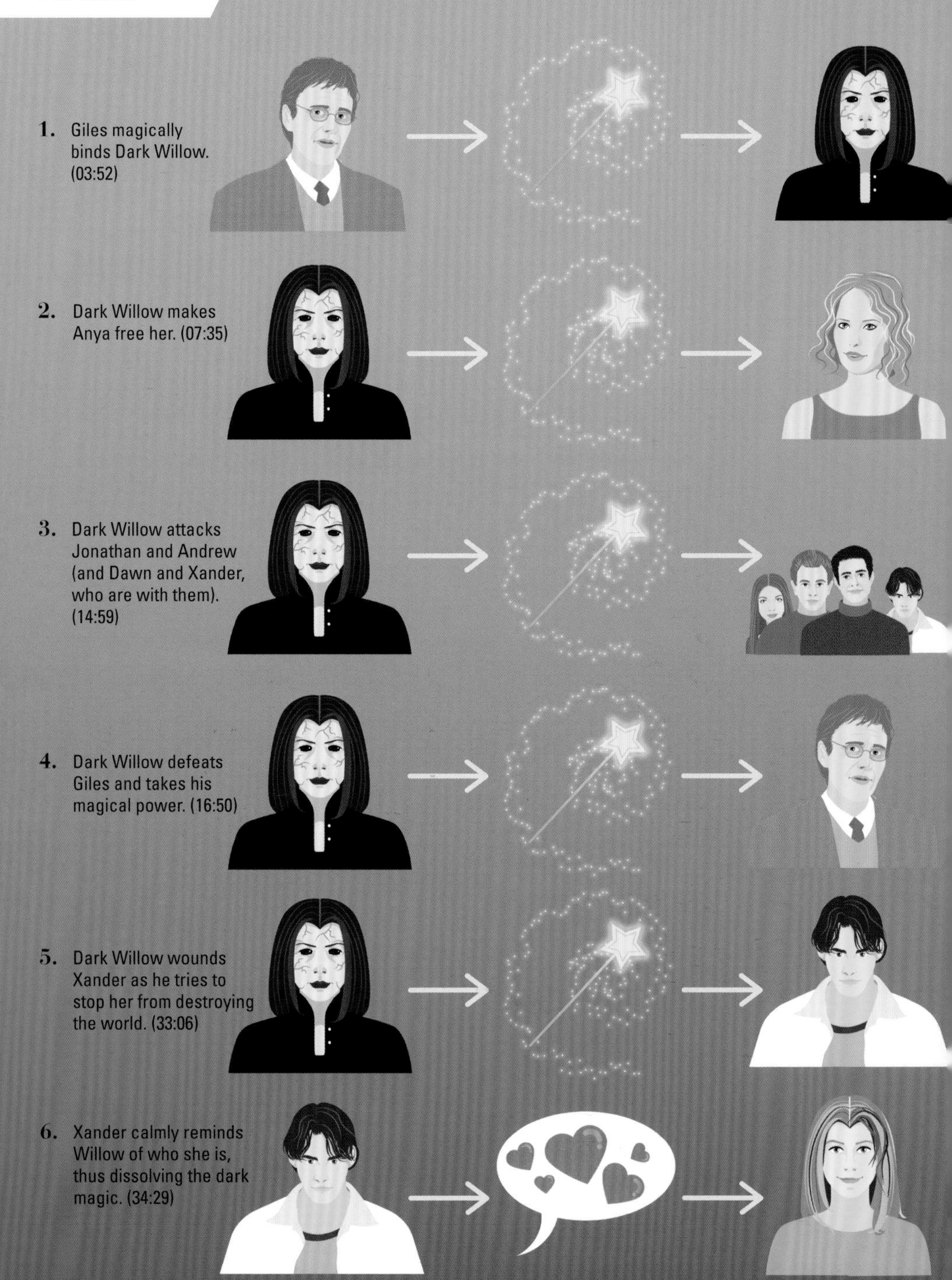

KEY DATES

1932

An earthquake swallows the satanic temple on Kingman's Bluff, dedicated to the demon Proserpexa.

2002

Tara Maclay is murdered. As a result of her grief, Willow turns to the dark side.

Glory finds Dawn.

THE HORROR, THE HORROR

Prior to the final battle, Willow has already hunted down, tortured, and skinned Warren

She lashes out at her friends, the police, and anyone else in her way

She inflicts wounds on Xander

THE HIGH COST OF WINNING

Giles almost dies using the coven's magic to battle against Dark Willow

FAITH LEHANE AND ANYA JENKINS

TWO KICKASS WOMEN, AT A GLANCE

TALENTS
Sex appeal
Fighting
Being BAD

HEIGHT
5'5"

FIRST WORDS
"S'okay, I got it. You're Buffy, right?"
3-03 Faith, Hope & Trick

LAST WORDS
"Yeah, you're not the one and only Chosen anymore. Just gotta live like a person. How's that feel?"
7-22 Chosen

ARM TATTOO

1998

Becomes the Slayer as a result of Kendra Young's death

Arrives in Sunnydale

1999

Accidentally kills Deputy Mayor Allan Finch

Forms an alliance with Mayor Richard Wilkins III

Murders a Sunnydale High geology professor

After Faith nearly kills Angel, Buffy stabs her and leaves her in a coma

ANYA EPISODE COUNT
85 (59%)

LOVES
Xander
Sex
Capitalism

HATES
Rabbits
Rabbits
Rabbits

PERSONALITY CHART

NOSTALGIC (FOR HER DAYS AS A DEMON) 15%
BLUNT 40%
LUSTFUL 45%

860
Born "Aud" in Sjornjost

880
Falls in love with Olaf, a Viking warrior

880/881
Is turned into a vengeance demon named Anyanka by D'Hoffryn

LOVES

Partying

Drinking

Having fun with guys

HATES

Pink

Being vulnerable

Dresses

20
(14%)

FAITH EPISODE COUNT

SOCIAL CIRCLE

FRIENDS
Mayor Wilkins

LOVERS
Xander Harris
Robin Wood

ENEMIES
Buffy Summers
Willow Rosenberg
Cordelia Chase
Rupert Giles
Angel
Spike
Anya Jenkins
Joyce Summers

2000
Reawakens from her coma

Switches bodies with Buffy with the help of a Draconian Katra

2003
Returns to Sunnydale and reconciles with Buffy

Is chosen as the leader of the potential Slayers

NICKNAMES

1 - The Rogue Slayer

2 - Slut-o-rama

3 - Miss Attention Span

TALENTS

Shopkeeping

Teleportation

Brutal honesty

BIRTHPLACE
Sweden

FIRST WORDS
"Nice bag. Prada?"
3-09 The Wish

LAST WORDS
"Bunnies! Floppy, hoppy bunnies."
7-22 Chosen

HEIGHT
5'3½"

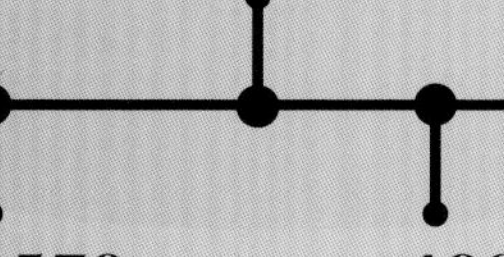

1579
Meets Count Dracula

1692
Attends the Salem witch trials

1998
Arrives in Sunnydale

Grants Cordelia's wish that Buffy had never come to Sunnydale

Giles destroys her necklace, making her mortal again

1999
Asks Xander to the school prom

2001
Gets engaged to Xander

2002
Xander leaves her at the altar, leading to the return of D'Hoffryn, who turns her into a vengeance demon once again

Has sex with Spike

Is stripped of her vengeance demon powers by D'Hoffryn

2003
Is nearly sliced in two by a Bringer's sword and dies

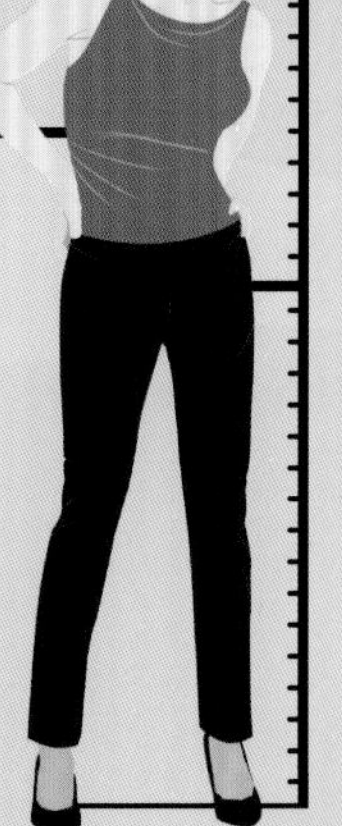

WANTED

POLICE DEPARTMENT OFFICIAL NOTICE

SUNNYDALE, CALIFORNIA

FAITH LEHANE

WANTED

FOR QUESTIONING CONCERNING

- criminal collusion with Mayor Richard Wilkins
- the murder of Deputy Mayor Allan Finch
- the attempted murder of a man known only as Angel
- body-switching
- kidnapping
- battery
- and other acts against the peace and dignity of Sunnydale.

By order of the State of California Police

SPIKE

WANTED

DEAD OR REALLY DEAD
FOR A NUMBER OF CRIMES, INCLUDING

- the massacre of the Kalderash Clan
- the murder of two Slayers
- the slaughter of an orphanage
- the murder of two honorable members of the Watchers' Council
- the kidnapping of Willow Rosenberg and Xander Harris

By order of the State of California Police

DARLA AND DRUSILLA

SAY HELLO TO THE FEMALE HALF OF THE DREADED WHIRLWIND

TALENTS
Seduction
Changing hairstyles
Being a good servant

HEIGHT
5′7″

FIRST WORDS
"Are you sure this is a good idea?"
1-01 Welcome to the Hellmouth

LAST WORDS
"Angel?"
1-07 Angel

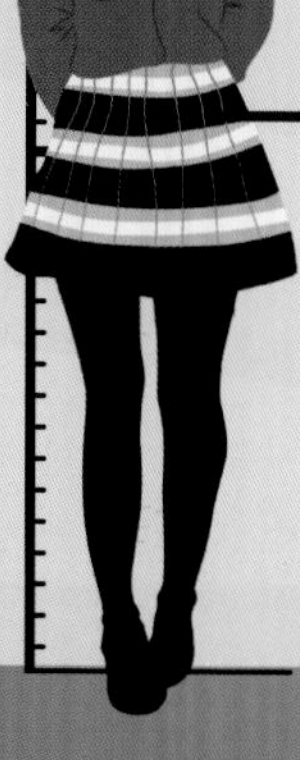

Late 16th century
Born in the British Isles

1609
Sired by the Master

1753
Sires Angel in Galway, Ireland

DRUSILLA EPISODE COUNT
17
(12%)

LOVES
Dolls
Plants
Torture

HATES
Red roses
Science
Acting like a grown-up

FASHION STYLE
- **1990s HEROINE CHIC 50%**
- **VICTORIAN COURTESAN 50%**

PERSONALITY CHART
- **IMMATURE 20%**
- **PSYCHOTIC 80%**

c. 1830
Born in the East End of London

1860
Meets Angelus and Darla

Angelus murders her family

1860s
Sired by Angelus

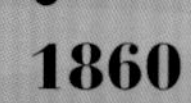

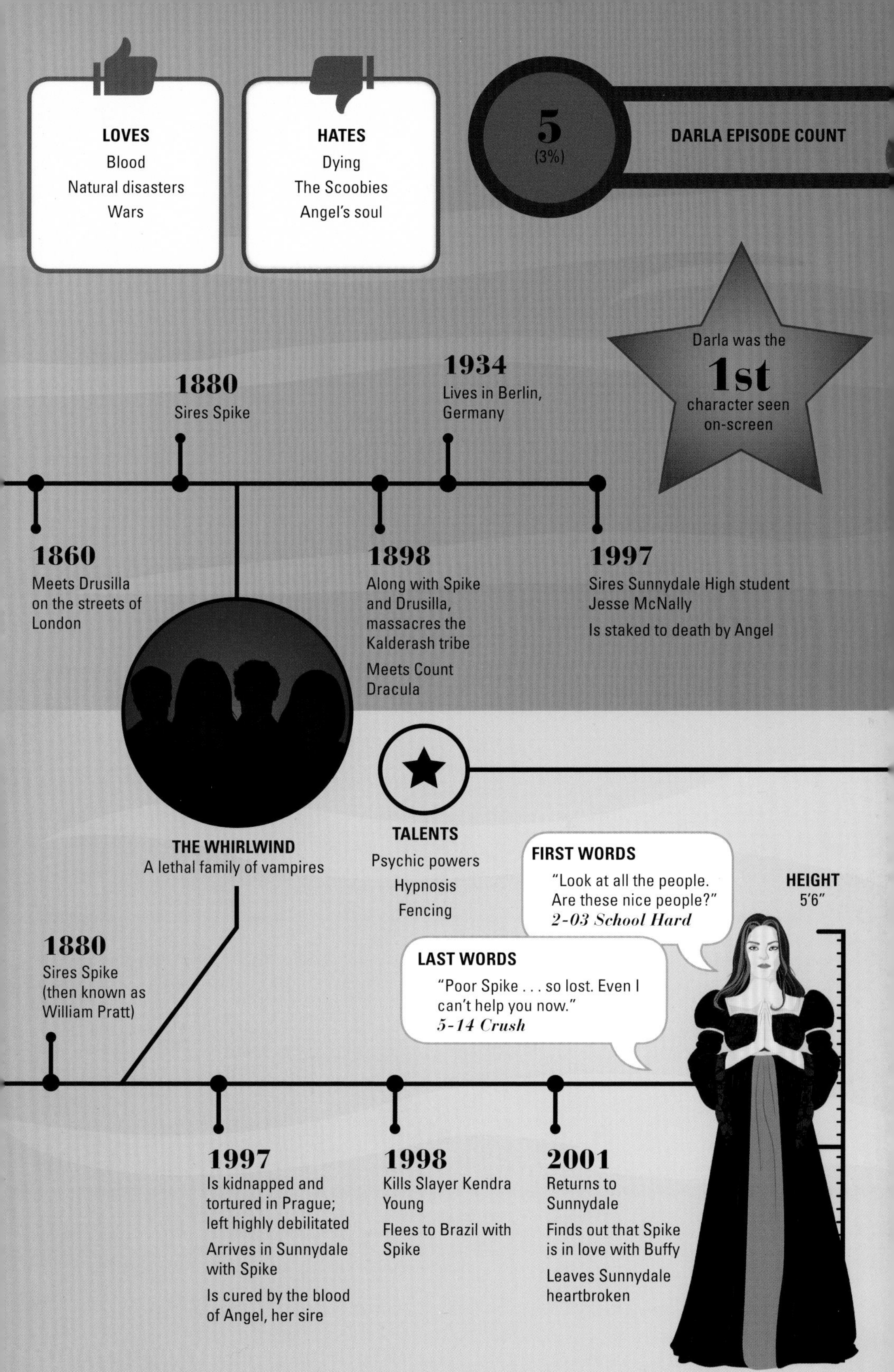
LOVES
Blood
Natural disasters
Wars
HATES
Dying
The Scoobies
Angel's soul
5
(3%)
DARLA EPISODE COUNT
Darla was the
1st
character seen
on-screen
1860
Meets Drusilla on the streets of London
1880
Sires Spike
1898
Along with Spike and Drusilla, massacres the Kalderash tribe
Meets Count Dracula
1934
Lives in Berlin, Germany
1997
Sires Sunnydale High student Jesse McNally
Is staked to death by Angel
THE WHIRLWIND
A lethal family of vampires
TALENTS
Psychic powers
Hypnosis
Fencing
FIRST WORDS
"Look at all the people. Are these nice people?"
2-03 School Hard
LAST WORDS
"Poor Spike . . . so lost. Even I can't help you now."
5-14 Crush
HEIGHT
5'6"
1880
Sires Spike (then known as William Pratt)
1997
Is kidnapped and tortured in Prague; left highly debilitated
Arrives in Sunnydale with Spike
Is cured by the blood of Angel, her sire
1998
Kills Slayer Kendra Young
Flees to Brazil with Spike
2001
Returns to Sunnydale
Finds out that Spike is in love with Buffy
Leaves Sunnydale heartbroken

WHO SIRED WHOM?

BUFFY: "THE WORD—WHEN YOU TURN A HUMAN INTO A VAMPIRE—IT'S—YOU 'SIRE' THEM."

HOLDEN: "COOL."

BUFFY: "IT'S A NOUN, TOO."

7-07 CONVERSATIONS WITH DEAD PEOPLE

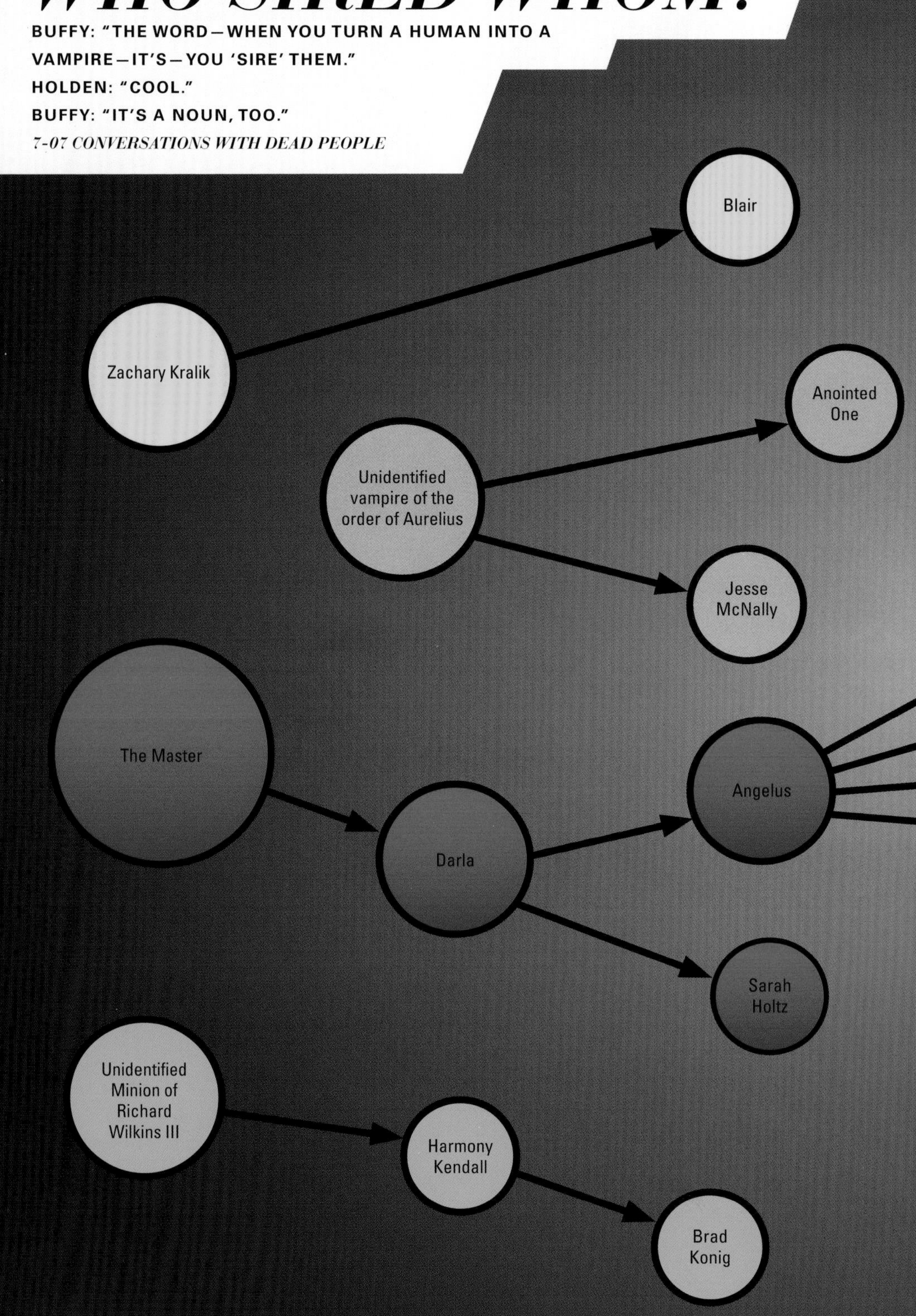

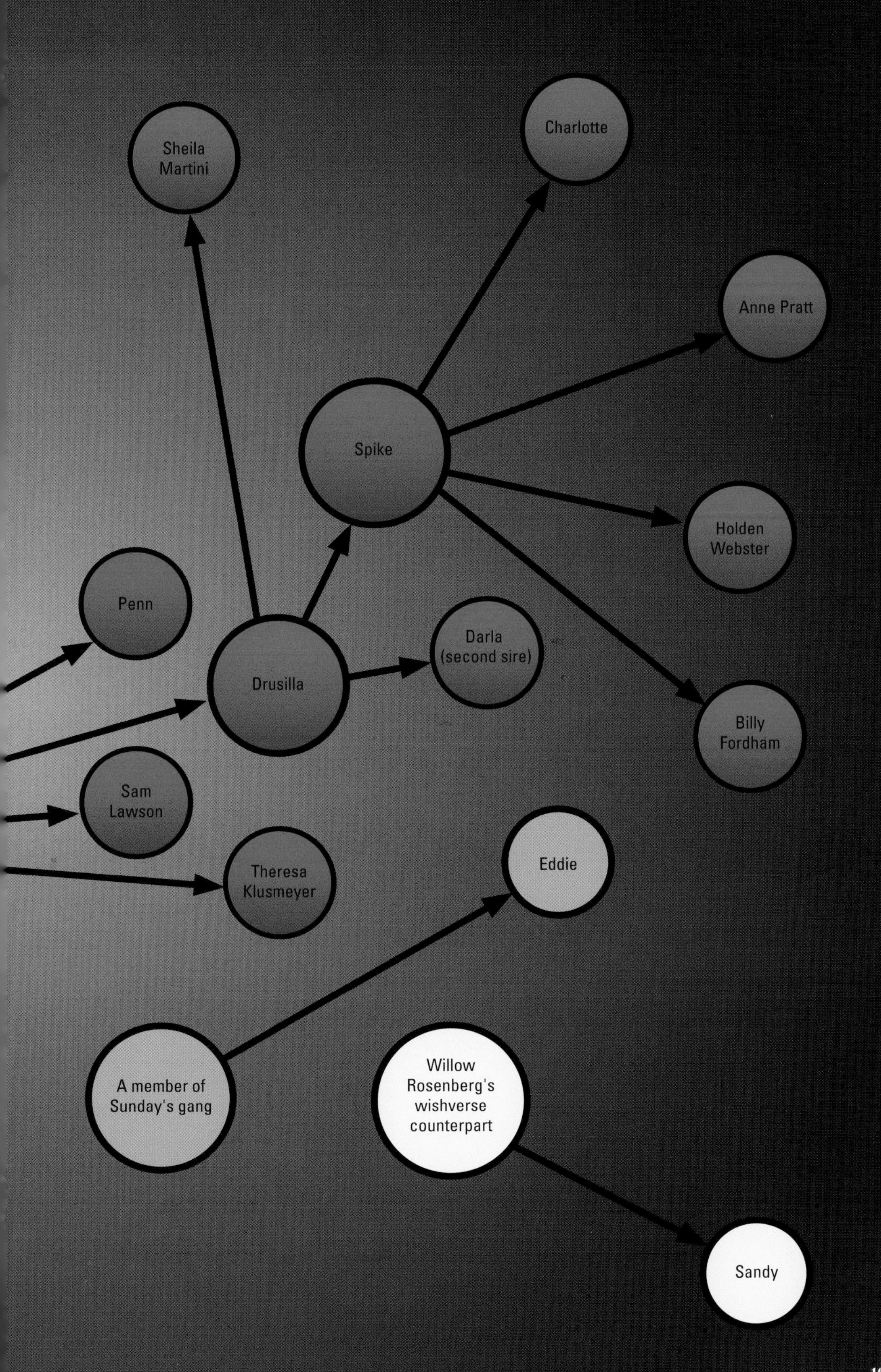
Sheila Martini
Charlotte
Anne Pratt
Spike
Holden Webster
Penn
Darla (second sire)
Drusilla
Billy Fordham
Sam Lawson
Theresa Klusmeyer
Eddie
A member of Sunday's gang
Willow Rosenberg's wishverse counterpart
Sandy

RESPECTING YOUR ELDERS

THERE ARE OLD ONES, AND THERE ARE *VERY* OLD ONES . . .

13.8 billion years ago

Beljoxa's Eye says that the First Evil has existed "since before the universe was born." Scientists estimate the universe to be some 13.8 billion years old. *7-11 Showtime*

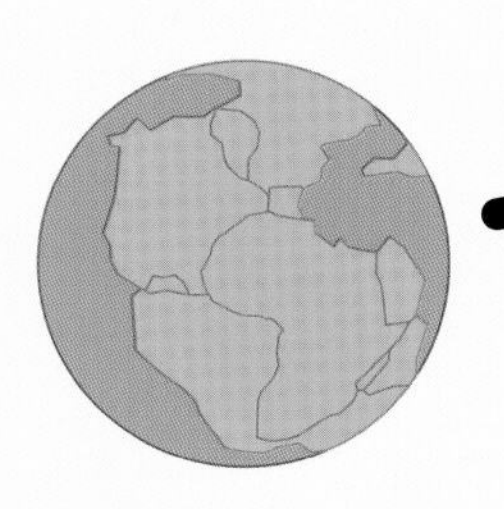

4.5 billions years ago

Scientists think the Earth is some 4.5 billion years old, but Giles says: "This world is older than any of you know."

He then explains the history of demons: For untold eons demons walked the Earth. They made it their home, their hell. But in time they lost their purchase on this reality. The way was made for mortal animals, for man. *1-02 The Harvest*

1100s

Dawn finds a passage in a book that says, "Tarnis, 12th century. One of the founders of the monks of the Order of Dagon. Their sole purpose appears to have been as protectors of the key." Does this suggest that Glorificus has been around since the 1100s, too? *5-13 Blood Ties*

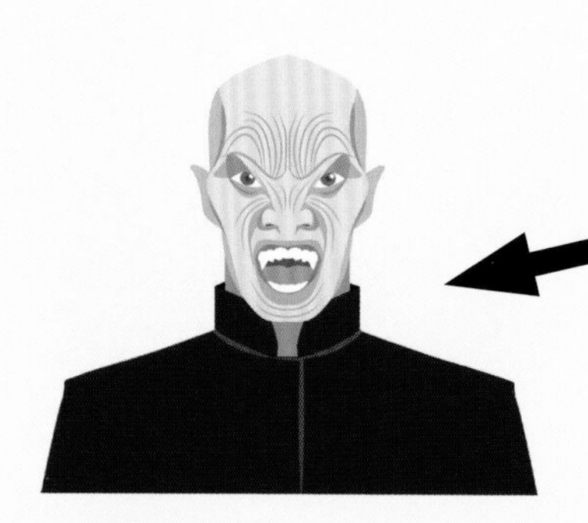

c. 1397

We're not told the age of the Master, but the shooting script of *1-01 Welcome to the Hellmouth* says he was "[b]orn Heinrich Joseph Nest (some six hundred years ago)."

On the DVD commentary for *1-02 The Harvest*, writer Joss Whedon says: "We decided early on that the Master would never be in normal face because he was so old and so far gone. We made him more animalistic than other vampires."

He says the Master has lived so long that he is "devolving." Could that also be true of Kakistos?

200,000–100,000 years ago

It is thought the first modern humans evolved in this period. According to Giles, these humans coexisted with the last of the Old Ones.

The books tell that the last demon to leave this reality fed off a human, mixing their blood. He was a human form possessed, infected by the demon's soul. He bit another and another, and so they walk the Earth, feeding, killing some, mixing their blood with others to make more of their kind. Waiting for the animals to die out and the Old Ones to return. ***1-02 The Harvest***

200,000–60,000 years ago

At an unknown date, three shamans—whom Buffy calls the Shadow Men—imbued a girl called Sineya with the energy, spirit, and heart of a demon. Sineya became the first Slayer.

In ***4-22 Restless***, Sineya says: "I have no speech."

Language is thought to have originated between 200,000 and 60,000 years ago. However, the Shadow Men seen in ***7-15 Get It Done*** speak, so perhaps they and Sineya are from the more recent past. Buffy can still communicate with Sineya in AD 2003.

[date unknown]

We're not told the age of the ancient vampire Kakistos, but he's "so old that his hands and feet are cloven" (***3-03 Faith, Hope & Trick***). He has an ancient Greek name. This may suggest he is thousands of years old.

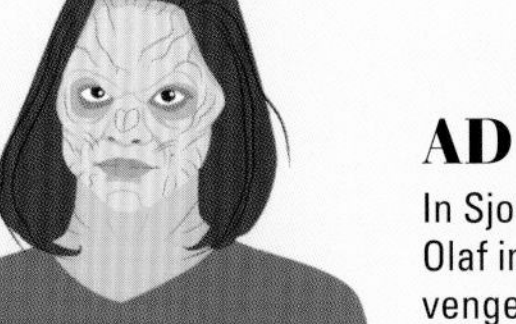

AD 880

In Sjornjost, Sweden, Aud transforms the unfaithful Olaf into a troll and accepts an offer to become the vengeance demon Anyanka. ***7-05 Selfless***

1418

The demon Moloch the Corruptor is trapped in the pages of a book in Cortona, Italy. He is freed again in Sunnydale in 1997, more than 500 years later. ***1-08 I, Robot . . . You, Jane***

c. 1428

Birth of Vlad III of Wallachia, whom Buffy later meets as the vampire Dracula. ***5-01 Buffy vs. Dracula***

BIG BATTLES— THE FIRST EVIL

7-22 CHOSEN

1. Buffy cuts Caleb in two with the M? scythe. (03:00)

2. Buffy leads Faith and the potential Slayers through the Seal of Danzalthar to face the Turok-Han vampires in the cavern below. (23:33)

3. Willow uses M? to turn all the Potentials into Slayers. (25:25)

4. The Slayers battle the Turok-Han vampires. (26:46)

5. Spike's soul and the amulet blast a hole up to the daylight and then direct sunshine into the cavern. (32:15)

6. Buffy and her surviving friends outrun the destruction of Sunnydale. (36:07)

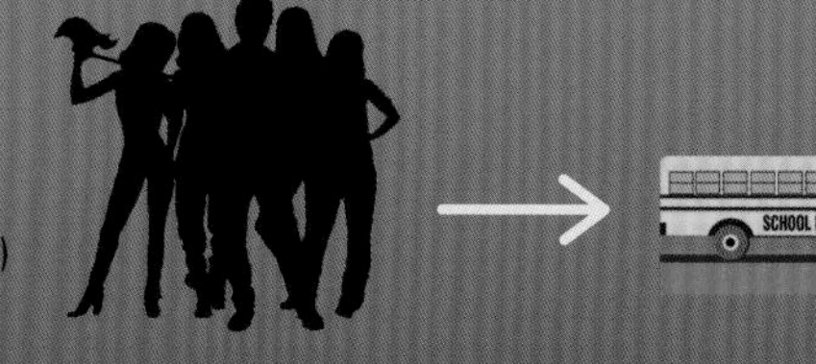

KEY DATES

Before the universe began
According to Beljoxa's Eye, the First Evil already existed.

1998 (Christmas)
The First almost convinces Angel to kill himself, but Angel changes his mind when it snows.

2001
Buffy's second resurrection creates instability in the line of Slayers, giving the First an opportunity to end it.

2002
The First appears to Andrew in Mexico and to Spike in Sunnydale, setting its plan in motion.

2003
Buffy foils the First's plan.

After the collapse of the universe
The First will still exist, apparently.

THE HORROR, THE HORROR

Buffy is stabbed through the chest with a sword and collapses

THE HIGH COST OF WINNING

Amanda, Anya, Spike, and many others die

Rona, Principal Wood, and many others are gravely wounded

Sunnydale is destroyed

WHAT HAPPENS NEXT, AFTER THE END OF THE SHOW?

Giles says there's a Hellmouth in Cleveland and that they have a lot of work ahead.

Willow says there are Slayers awakening everywhere, and Dawn says they should find them.

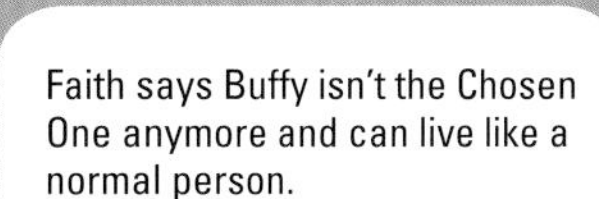

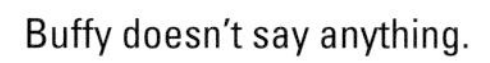

THE TRIO (JONATHAN LEVINSON, WARREN MEARS, AND ANDREW WELLS)

"SO YOU THREE HAVE WHAT? BANDED TOGETHER TO BE PAINS IN MY ASS?"

—BUFFY, *6-11 GONE*

1997
Cordelia picks Jonathan to take her to the prom

1998
Jonathan becomes possessed by a Bezoar

1999
Jonathan plans to commit suicide at the top of the school's bell tower

TALENTS
N/A

LOVES
Being in a gang
Girls
Being liked

JONATHAN

FIRST WORDS
"Your hands feel kind of . . . rough."
2-04 Inca Mummy Girl

LAST WORDS
"Well, I still care about them. That's why I'm here."
7-07 Conversations with Dead People

HATES
Bullies
Being short
Being bossed around

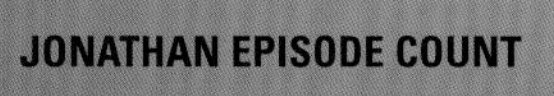

JONATHAN EPISODE COUNT

28
(19%)

LOVES
Science fiction
Collecting
Comic books

HATES
Bullies
Reality
Being bossed around

25 (17%) **ANDREW EPISODE COUNT**

FIRST WORDS
"We can do that."
6-04 Flooded

LAST WORDS
"She was incredible. She died saving my life."
7-22 Chosen

TALENTS
Organization
Pop-culture knowledge
Surviving

ANDREW

2000
Jonathan casts a spell that makes everyone in Sunnydale think he is a superstar

2001
Jonathan meets Warren and Andrew
As the Trio, they hire a demon to rob a bank and attack Buffy
The Trio steals the Illuminata diamond from the Sunnydale Museum of Natural History

2002
Warren steals the Orbs of Nezzla'Khan
Jonathan and Andrew are arrested, while Warren escapes
Warren kills Tara
Willow kills Warren
Jonathan and Andrew escape to Mexico
Jonathan and Andrew return to Sunnydale
While under the spell of the First Evil, Andrew stabs Jonathan to death
Anya saves Andrew's life

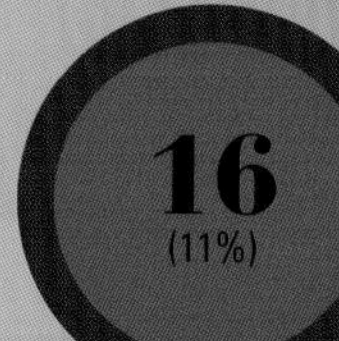

16 (11%) **WARREN EPISODE COUNT**

FIRST WORDS
"We gotta go, she's gonna see me."
5-15 I Was Made To Love You

LAST WORDS
"Oh, and when you get caught, you'll lose them too. Your friends. You don't want that. I know you're in pain, but—"
6-20 Villains

LOVES
Robot girls
Being a villain
Killing

HATES
Real girls
Buffy
Frankie the Jock

TALENTS
Gadget-building
Stealing stuff
Bossing Andrew and Jonathan around

WARREN

NERD SHELF

A QUICK LOOK AT ANDREW'S COLLECTION

BOOKS

Misery

Harry Potter and the Sorcerer's Stone

DVDS

Ocean's Eleven

Back to the Future

Star Wars trilogy

The X-Files

James Bond

Babe

Red Dwarf

SpongeBob Squarepants

Babylon 5

Ghost

Dragon Ball Z

Hellraiser

Dr. Strangelove

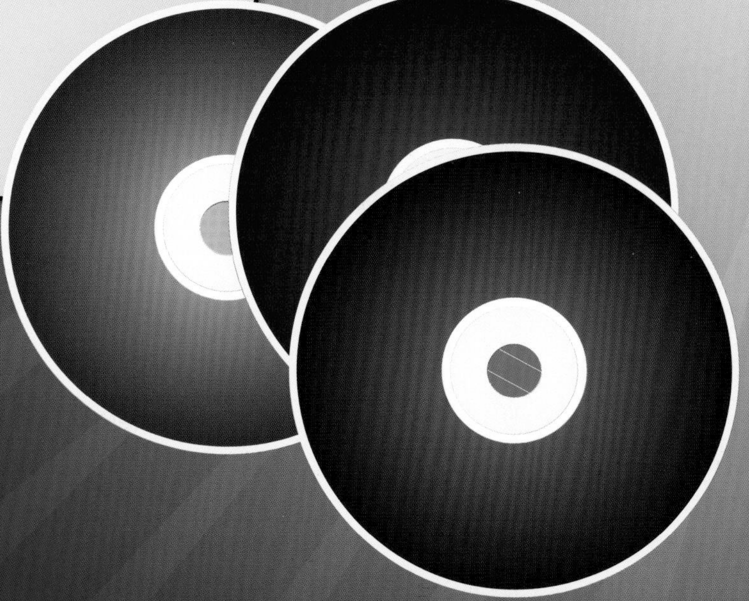

ARCADE GAMES
Dead or Alive
#24
COMICS
X-Men
Justice League
The League of Extraordinary Gentlemen
The Incredible Hulk
Captain America
8
8
7
ROLE-PLAYING GAMES
Dungeons and Dragons

BUFFY AND POP CULTURE

OVER SEVEN SEASONS, BUFFY AND HER FRIENDS NAME-CHECK MANY CULTURAL ICONS. HERE ARE JUST A FEW . . .

CRITICS

Roger Ebert
Gene Siskel

PLAYS

Death of a Salesman
Hamlet
Julius Caesar
The Merchant of Venice
The Rocky Horror Picture Show

COMEDIANS

Buster Keaton
The Three Stooges
The Marx Brothers

MOVIES

Abbott and Costello Meet Frankenstein
Apocalypse Now
Babe: Pig in the City
Back to the Future
The Bad Seed
Bill and Ted's Bogus Journey
The Blair Witch Project
Blue Lagoon
Cocktail
Conan the Destroyer
Creature from the Black Lagoon
Dracula (1973)
The English Patient
The Empire Strikes Back
The Evil Dead
The Exorcist
Fantasia
Faster, Pussycat! Kill! Kill!
First Blood
Frankenstein
The Fury
The Full Monty
Ghostbusters
Glitter
Godzilla
Gone with the Wind
The Graduate
Hellraiser
Highlander
The Hunchback of Notre Dame
Indiana Jones and the Temple of Doom
James Bond films
Jaws
Jaws 3-D
The Lost Weekend
The Little Rascals
JFK
Magnolia
Marathon Man
Mary Poppins
The Matrix
Misery
Miss Congeniality
Mommie Dearest
Moulin Rouge!
My Fair Lady
The Phantom Menace
Planet of the Apes
Ocean's Eleven
One Million Years B.C.
Poltergeist
Pretty in Pink
Private Benjamin
Pump Up the Volume
Return of the Jedi
The Seventh Seal
Signs
Sleepless in Seattle
The Shining
The Sound of Music
Steel Magnolias
The Stepford Wives
This Is Spinal Tap
Thelma & Louise
The Terminator
The Usual Suspects
The Wedding Planner
The Wild Bunch
Witness

POEMS

"The Death of the Hired Man"
"Marmion"
"Stopping by Woods on a Snowy Evening"

OPERA
Don Giovanni
Madame Butterfly

WRITERS
Maya Angelou
Samuel Beckett
Helen Keller
Ernest Hemingway
Anne Rice

COMICS
The Avengers
Batman
Captain America
The Incredible Hulk
Justice League
The League of Extraordinary Gentlemen
Spider-Man
Superman
Super Friends
Wonder Woman
X-Men

MAGAZINES
Esquire
Reader's Digest
Vanity Fair

BOOKS
The Call of the Wild
The Cask of Amontillado
A Christmas Carol
The Deep End of the Ocean
Harry Potter
The Lord of the Rings
Nausea
Rebecca of Sunnybrook Farm
Sherlock Holmes
1984
Of Human Bondage
On the Road
Strange Case of Dr. Jekyll and Mr. Hyde
Uncle Tom's Cabin
The Vampire Chronicles

ACTORS
Kevin Bacon
Antonio Banderas
Humphrey Bogart
Matthew Broderick
Chevy Chase
George Clooney
Tom Cruise
Ellen DeGeneres
Marlene Dietrich
Farrah Fawcett
Nicole Kidman
Gwyneth Paltrow
Christina Ricci
Molly Ringwald
James Spader
Charlize Theron
John Wayne

DIRECTORS
Ken Russell

TV
The A-Team
The Addams Family
Babylon 5
Candid Camera
Charlie's Angels
A Charlie Brown Christmas
CSI
Dawson's Creek
Doctor Who
Doogie Howser, M.D.
Dragnet
ER
Falcon Crest
Gentle Ben
H.R. Pufnstuf
Jeopardy
Knight Rider
Looney Tunes
The Lone Ranger
Manimal
Mighty Morphin Power Rangers
Mighty Mouse
Monty Python's Flying Circus
Mr. Belvedere
Murder, She Wrote
Nightline
The Oprah Winfrey Show
Oz
Passions
The Prisoner
The Real World
Red Dwarf
Scooby-Doo, Where Are You!
Sesame Street
The Simpsons
SpongeBob SquarePants
Star Trek
Star Trek: Enterprise
Star Trek: The Next Generation
Super Friends
Teletubbies
The X-Files
Walker, Texas Ranger
War Games
Wheel of Fortune
Xena: Warrior Princess

PAINTERS
Claude Monet
Gustav Klimt
Vincent van Gogh
Grant Wood

WHAT'S MY LINE?

CHARACTERS NAMING THE EPISODE THEY'RE IN

1-02 The Harvest The Master: "She mustn't be allowed to interfere with the Harvest!"

1-03 Witch Giles: "This witch is casting horrible and disfiguring spells . . ."

1-06 The Pack Zookeeper: "Once they separate him, the pack devours them."

1-07 Angel Willow: "What about Angel?"

1-10 Nightmares Wendell Sears: "That's when the nightmares started."

2-05 Reptile Boy Buffy: "Hey, reptile boy!"

2-06 Halloween Willow: "Snyder must be in charge of the volunteer safety program for Halloween this year."

2-07 Lie to Me Buffy: "And don't lie to me."

2-09 What's My Line (Part 1) Buffy: "Well, then you know it's a whole week of *What's My Line?*"

2-11 Ted Joyce: "Buffy, this is Ted."

2-13 Surprise Buffy: "Surprise me."

2-15 Phases Giles: "The phases of the moon do seem to exert a great deal of psychological influence."

2-17 Passion Angelus: "Passion."

3-01 Anne Rickie Thomas: "I think we're good, um, Anne."

3-02 Dead Man's Party Oz: "I think the dead man's party moved upstairs."

3-05 Homecoming Willow: "And it is our last Homecoming Dance."

3-06 Band Candy Principal Snyder: "It's band candy."

3-10 Amends Buffy: "Angel, you have the power to do real good, to make amends."

3-11 Gingerbread Xander: "Breadcrumbs, ovens, gingerbread house?"

3-12 Helpless Buffy: "What if I just hide under my bed, all scared and helpless?"

3-13 The Zeppo Cordelia: "You're the Zeppo."

3-19 Choices Joyce: "I'm just so pleased that you have so many choices."

3-20 The Prom Buffy: "Like after the prom."

4-05 Beer Bad Xander: "Beer bad."

4-07 The Initiative Professor Walsh: "Fail to recapture it and everything we've worked for–the Initiative itself–could end tonight."

4-11 Doomed Buffy: "It's just doomed."

4-16 Who Are You? Buffy (in Faith's body): "Who are you?"

4-20 The Yoko Factor Spike: "It's called the Yoko factor."

4-21 Primeval Buffy: "Messing with primeval forces you have absolutely no comprehension of."

5-02 Real Me Dawn: "Nobody knows who I am, not the real me."

5-06 Family Intern: "Got her family out there."

5-08 Shadow Joyce: "A shadow."

5-14 Crush Buffy: "You have a crush on him."

5-16 The Body 911 operator (a telephone): "The body's cold?"

5-17 Forever Dawn: "She's the one who has to be in it forever."

5-18 Intervention Willow: "Intervention time again?"

6-04 Flooded Spike: "Did you know this place was flooded?"

6-06 All the Way Zack: "But what about, you know, going all the way?"

6-07 Once More, with Feeling Sweet: "Say you're happy now, once more with feeling."

6-08 Tabula Rasa Willow: "Tabula rasa, tabula rasa, tabula rasa."

6-11 Gone Spike: "Yeah, well, the fact is my lighter's gone missing."

6-21 Two to Go Anya: "So we're talking about 'two to go,' right—Jonathan and whatshisface, the other guy?"

6-22 Grave Buffy: "It was like when I clawed my way out of that grave."

7-02 Beneath You German girl: "From beneath you it devours."

7-04 Help Xander: "I wanna help."

7-06 Him Buffy: "The school basement is making him crazy."

7-09 Never Leave Me Spike: "Oh, never leave me."

7-11 Showtime Willow: "It's showtime."

7-12 Potential Giles: "Potential Slayers."

7-20 Touched Robin Wood: "We all want someone who cares, to be touched that way."

7-22 Chosen Buffy: "I hate that there's evil and that I was chosen to fight it."

SUNNYDALE HALL OF FAME

A ROUNDUP OF ACTORS WITH MINOR ROLES IN THE SHOW WHO WENT ON TO BECOME STARS

(Beth Maclay, *5-06 Family*)
Arrival
American Hustle
Man of Steel

(Billy Fordham, *2-07 Lie to Me*)
Dawson's Creek
The Grudge

(Colleen, *7-18 Dirty Girls*)
The O.C.

(Vi, *7-11 Showtime*)*
Supernatural
Dr. Horrible's Sing-Along Blog
The Guild

(Lissa, *7-14 First Date*)
Grammy Award–winning singer
John Tucker Must Die
The Muppets' Wizard of Oz

(Marcie Ross, *1-11 Out of Mind, Out of Sight*)
Argo
Carnivàle
Girl, Interrupted

(George, *2-19 I Only Have Eyes for You*)
Lincoln
The Sessions
Deadwood

(Caleb, *7-18 Dirty Girls*)*
Castle
Serenity
Firefly

(Hunt, *4-05 Beer Bad*)
Harold and Kumar

* First appearance.

EPISODE-BY-EPISODE GUIDE

AN OVERVIEW OF RATINGS AND RANKINGS FOR THE WHOLE SHOW

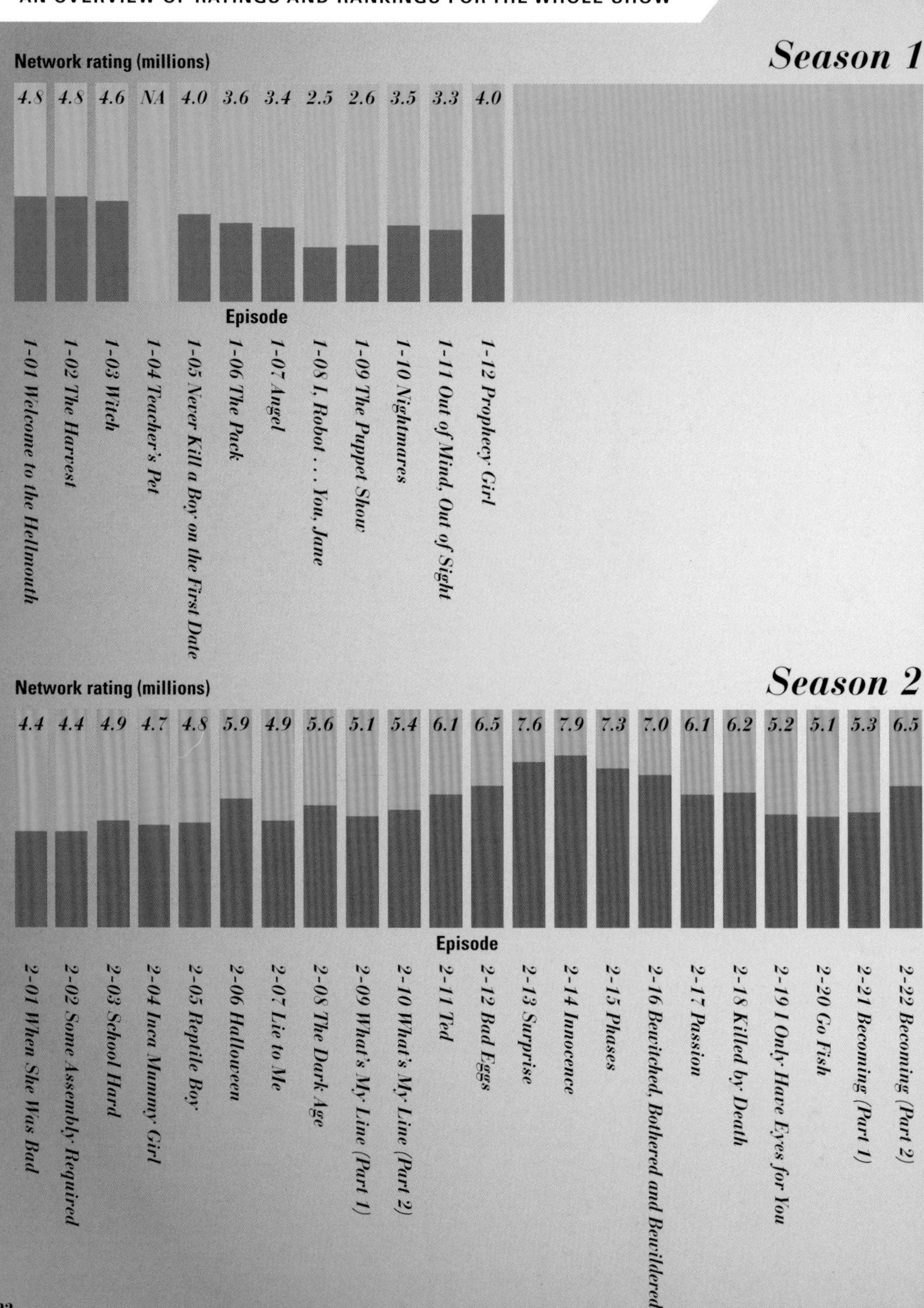

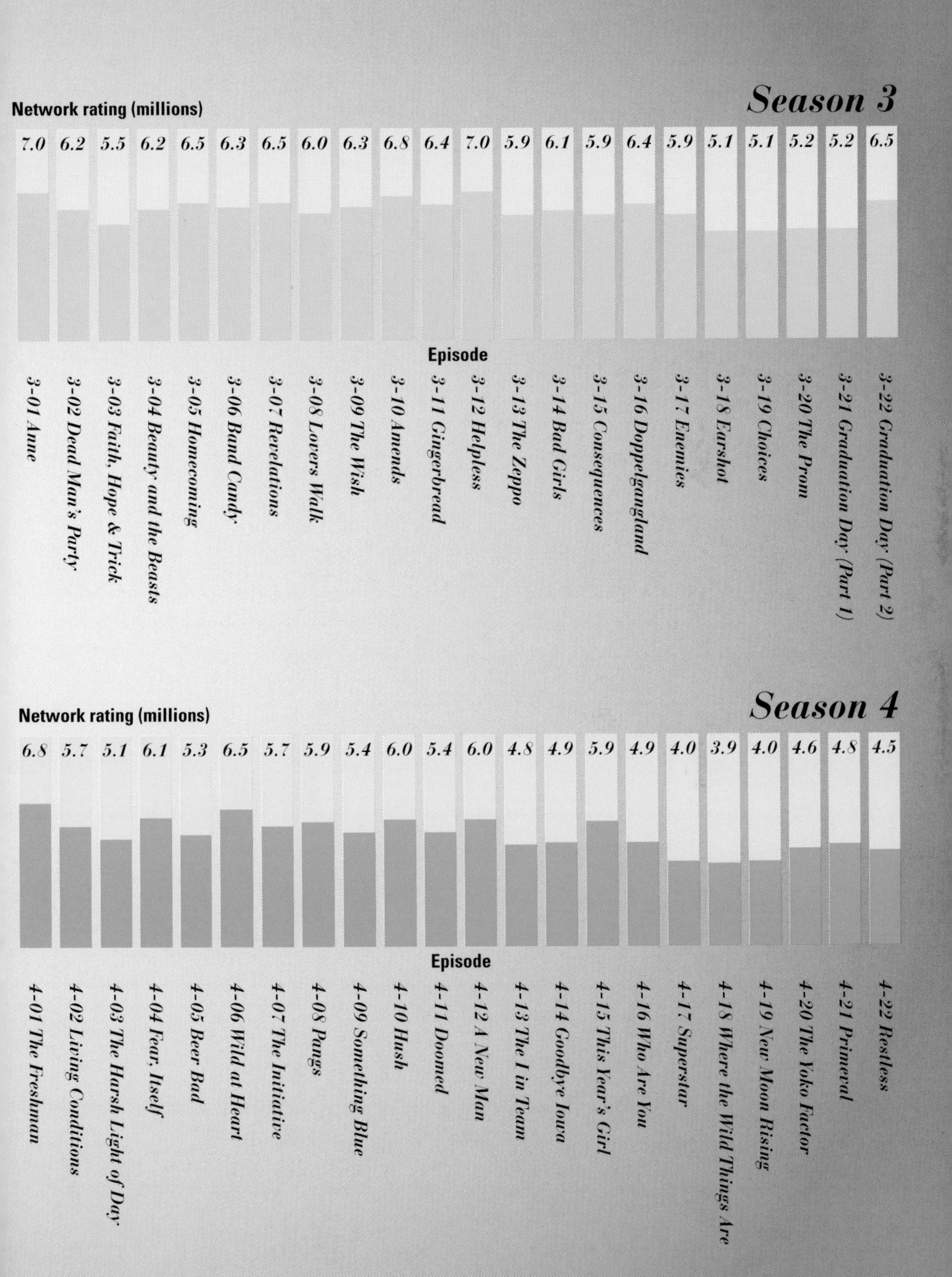
Season 3
Network rating (millions)
7.0
6.2
5.5
6.2
6.5
6.3
6.5
6.0
6.3
6.8
6.4
7.0
5.9
6.1
5.9
6.4
5.9
5.1
5.1
5.2
5.2
6.5
Episode
3-01 Anne
3-02 Dead Man's Party
3-03 Faith, Hope & Trick
3-04 Beauty and the Beasts
3-05 Homecoming
3-06 Band Candy
3-07 Revelations
3-08 Lovers Walk
3-09 The Wish
3-10 Amends
3-11 Gingerbread
3-12 Helpless
3-13 The Zeppo
3-14 Bad Girls
3-15 Consequences
3-16 Doppelgangland
3-17 Enemies
3-18 Earshot
3-19 Choices
3-20 The Prom
3-21 Graduation Day (Part 1)
3-22 Graduation Day (Part 2)
Season 4
Network rating (millions)
6.8
5.7
5.1
6.1
5.3
6.5
5.7
5.9
5.4
6.0
5.4
6.0
4.8
4.9
5.9
4.9
4.0
3.9
4.0
4.6
4.8
4.5
Episode
4-01 The Freshman
4-02 Living Conditions
4-03 The Harsh Light of Day
4-04 Fear, Itself
4-05 Beer Bad
4-06 Wild at Heart
4-07 The Initiative
4-08 Pangs
4-09 Something Blue
4-10 Hush
4-11 Doomed
4-12 A New Man
4-13 The I in Team
4-14 Goodbye Iowa
4-15 This Year's Girl
4-16 Who Are You
4-17 Superstar
4-18 Where the Wild Things Are
4-19 New Moon Rising
4-20 The Yoko Factor
4-21 Primeval
4-22 Restless

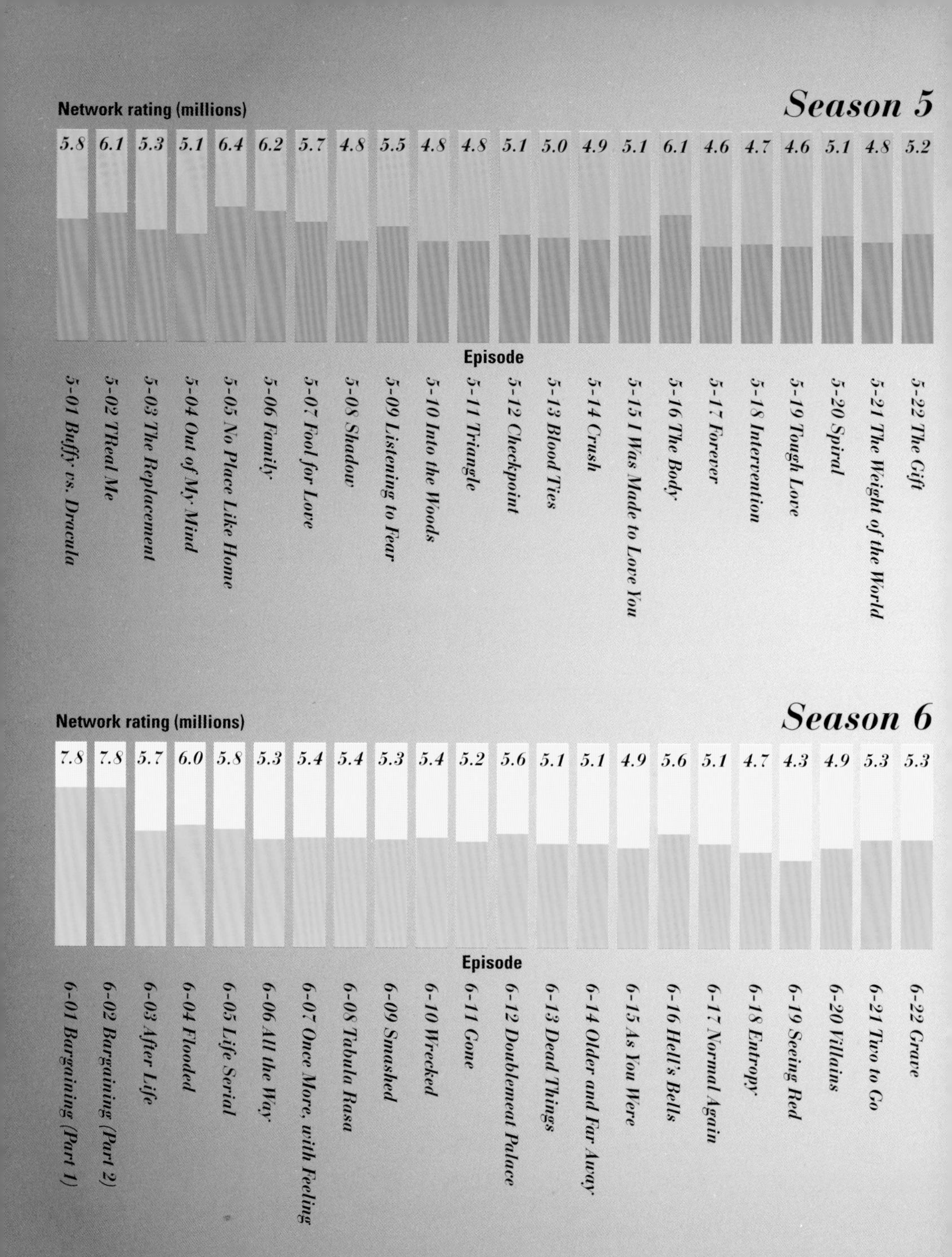

Network rating (millions)
Season 5
5.8
6.1
5.3
5.1
6.4
6.2
5.7
4.8
5.5
4.8
4.8
5.1
5.0
4.9
5.1
6.1
4.6
4.7
4.6
5.1
4.8
5.2
Episode
5-01 Buffy vs. Dracula
5-02 Real Me
5-03 The Replacement
5-04 Out of My Mind
5-05 No Place Like Home
5-06 Family
5-07 Fool for Love
5-08 Shadow
5-09 Listening to Fear
5-10 Into the Woods
5-11 Triangle
5-12 Checkpoint
5-13 Blood Ties
5-14 Crush
5-15 I Was Made to Love You
5-16 The Body
5-17 Forever
5-18 Intervention
5-19 Tough Love
5-20 Spiral
5-21 The Weight of the World
5-22 The Gift
Network rating (millions)
Season 6
7.8
7.8
5.7
6.0
5.8
5.3
5.4
5.4
5.3
5.4
5.2
5.6
5.1
5.1
4.9
5.6
5.1
4.7
4.3
4.9
5.3
5.3
Episode
6-01 Bargaining (Part 1)
6-02 Bargaining (Part 2)
6-03 After Life
6-04 Flooded
6-05 Life Serial
6-06 All the Way
6-07 Once More, with Feeling
6-08 Tabula Rasa
6-09 Smashed
6-10 Wrecked
6-11 Gone
6-12 Doublemeat Palace
6-13 Dead Things
6-14 Older and Far Away
6-15 As You Were
6-16 Hell's Bells
6-17 Normal Again
6-18 Entropy
6-19 Seeing Red
6-20 Villains
6-21 Two to Go
6-22 Grave

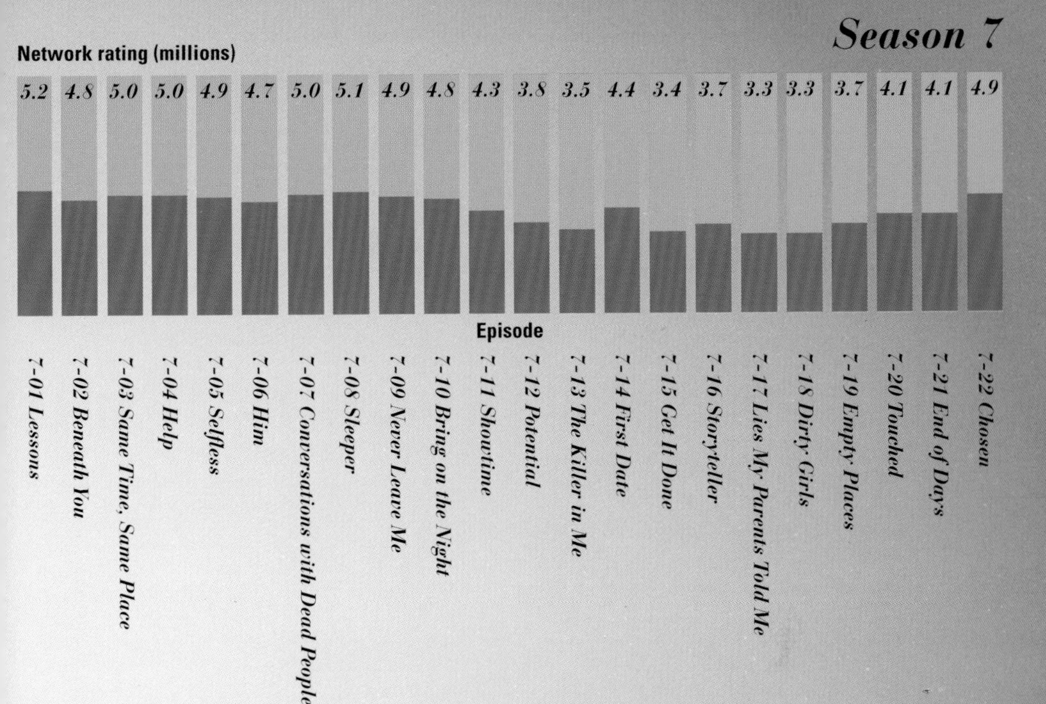

2-14 Innocence

WINNER of Emmy for Outstanding Makeup for a Series

2-21 Becoming (Part 1)

WINNER of Emmy for Outstanding Music Composition for a Series

4-05 Beer Bad

NOMINATED for Emmy for Outstanding Hairstyling for a Series

4-10 Hush

NOMINATED for Emmys for Outstanding Cinematography for a Single Camera Series and for Outstanding Writing for a Drama Series

5-16 The Body

NOMINATED for Nebula Award for Best Script

6-07 Once More, with Feeling

NOMINATED for Emmy for Outstanding Music Direction, for Hugo Award for Best Dramatic Presentation, and for Nebula Award for Best Script

6-16 Hell's Bells

NOMINATED for Emmys for Outstanding Hairstyling for a Series, for Outstanding Makeup (non-prosthetic) for a Series, and for Outstanding Makeup (prosthetic) for a Series

7-07 Conversations with Dead People

WINNER of Hugo Award for Best Dramatic Presentation, Short Form

7-22 Chosen

NOMINATED for Emmy for Outstanding Special Visual Effects for a Series, and for Hugo Award for Best Dramatic Presentation, Short Form

ACKNOWLEDGMENTS

Thanks to the cast and crew of *Buffy the Vampire Slayer*—not that they were directly involved in this book, but for giving us so much to sink our fangs into. We're also very grateful to everyone at 20th Century Fox and the team at Insight Editions for their generosity and patience.

Simon would like to thank Samira Ahmed, Simon Belcher, Debbie Challis, Jessica Eastwood, and Gemma Romain.

Steve would like to thank Britt O'Brien, Lizzie Rogers, Jayne Nelson, and Alex Drew.

www.insighteditions.com

Find us on Facebook:
www.facebook.com/InsightEditions

Follow us on Twitter: @insighteditions

Library of Congress Cataloging-in-Publication Data available.

ISBN: 978-1-68383-056-6

Publisher: Raoul Goff
Associate Publisher: Vanessa Lopez
Art Director: Chrissy Kwasnik
Senior Designer: Stuart Smith
Senior Editor: Rossella Barry
Managing Editor: Alan Kaplan
Senior Production Editor: Rachel Anderson
Editorial Assistant: Tessa Murphy
Production Manager: Sam Taylor

Illustrations by Ilaria Vescovo, Tomato Farm Agency

Insight Editions would like to thank Laura Kavanagh for her important editorial help.

REPLANTED PAPER

Insight Editions, in association with Roots of Peace, will plant two trees for each tree used in the manufacturing of this book. Roots of Peace is an internationally renowned humanitarian organization dedicated to eradicating land mines worldwide and converting war-torn lands into productive farms and wildlife habitats. Roots of Peace will plant two million fruit and nut trees in Afghanistan and provide farmers there with the skills and support necessary for sustainable land use.

Manufactured in China by Insight Editions

10 9 8 7 6 5 4 3 2 1